DO
WE NEED
THE CHURCH?

DO
WE NEED
THE CHURCH?

Richard P. McBrien

1817

Harper & Row, Publishers
New York and Evanston

Library of Congress Catalog Card Number: 69-10476

M-T

For my colleagues and students at
Pope John XXIII National Seminary
and in memory of its patron

Preface

Undoubtedly there are Catholic theologians with older and wiser heads than mine who should have written this book. But they did not. And I did. I am sure that I shall be hearing from them in comment and review. If the book accomplishes nothing more than the stimulation of a frank and open discussion of the whole question of the place and function of the Christian Church, then it will have achieved a significant end.

I am hopeful that the basic argument of this book will be welcomed by many Christians, and particularly by Roman Catholics. This is not the first time that I have proposed these ideas. I have published them in various forms in the Catholic Press; I have offered them in several public lectures; I have discussed them with my seminary and university colleagues and students; and I have presented them to large audiences of Catholic priests in at least six dioceses as well as to a military chaplains' group. The response, especially from those engaged in the pastoral ministry, has been profoundly encouraging. Many displayed genuine enthusiasm when I assured them that I was under contract to collect these ideas in book form.

These experiences have strengthened in my own mind the force of Pope John XXIII's statement in his encyclical letter, *Ad Petri Cathedram* (a text which serves as a kind of extended motto for the *Quaestiones Disputatae* series[1]): 'There are many points which the Church leaves to the discussion of theologians, in that there is no absolute certainty about them. As the eminent Cardinal Newman remarked, such controversies do not disrupt the Church's unity; rather they contribute greatly to a deeper and better understanding of her dogmas. These very differences shed in effect a new light on the Church's teaching, and pave and fortify the way to the attainment of unity.'

Even the limited achievements of the Second Vatican Council would have been unthinkable without the spirit of Pope John's openness toward theological discussion. I say 'limited achievements' because I am convinced that Vatican II did not go nearly far enough. I realize that some Catholics are having great difficulty simply catching up with the council, but we can no longer afford the luxury of waiting for the gap to close.

As Cardinal Suenens of Belgium said at the recent Congress of the Theology of the Renewal of the Church at Toronto (August 22, 1967), the unanimity of opinion at Vatican II was purchased at a high price.

> In the conciliar texts [he stated] there are some formulae whose aim was to counterbalance other assertions, or to win wider assent; these were, in some cases, like temporary stopping places in a long climb. Because of the interplay of circumstances—and of men—certain emphases did not manage to have their full force for renewal. But the seeds are there, like unopened buds awaiting the sun: it will be the task of men moved by the Holy Spirit to draw out all the vital riches contained in the conciliar texts—and, for that matter, in all that was said both inside and outside the Council hall, but which has become an integral part of Vatican II.

This book takes the risk of opening buds.

RICHARD P. McBRIEN
Pope John XXIII National Seminary, Weston, Massachusetts

Contents

Part Four

TOWARD A NEW THEOLOGY OF THE CHURCH

Introduction

This is a book about the Christian Church, and it is written out of the conviction, undoubtedly arrogant in appearance, that most Christians do not know what the Church is and what mission it has to fulfill. By the Church I mean the community of those who profess explicit faith in the Lordship of Jesus Christ and who have ratified this faith in baptism.[2] To profess faith in the Lordship of Christ is to share the historic conviction that in the life, death, and resurrection of Jesus of Nazareth reside the ultimate meaning of human existence and of all history. Even though this latter affirmation may sound ponderously evangelical and irremediably sectarian, it is not meant to be so, and the fuller secular meaning of the Lordship of Christ should gradually emerge as the argument of the book is progressively constructed.

This book is essentially a critique of the *traditional* theology of the Church, and I include the Second Vatican Council under that same adjectival umbrella. Its concerns are at least as large as the Church itself, which means that Protestantism, Eastern Orthodoxy, and Anglicanism are as much included in the discussion as Roman Catholicism. It will be inevitable, however, that the Roman Catholic Church should be the point of reference most frequently.

This inquiry into the nature and mission of the Church is motivated by the conviction that the meaning and place of the Church is the most practical and urgent question facing Christians in our time. This judgment will appear to conflict with a prevailing belief, especially among some

Protestant theologians, that the problem of God, not the Church, has theological and pastoral priority. I do not mean to imply here that ecclesiology is the most important area of Christian theology. I shall argue throughout this book that it is impossible to understand the mission of the Church apart from the mission of Jesus himself, and that it is, furthermore, impossible to understand his mission without reference to the Kingdom of God. Ecclesiology, therefore, must presuppose responsible probings into Christology and the problem of God.

Nevertheless, I agree with Robert Adolfs that the problem of God is more probably 'a symptom of a crisis in the churches',[3] although I should insist that the 'crisis in the churches' goes far deeper than the problem of the Church's form and the conservative character of ecclesiastical institutions.[4] The ultimate issue is theological, and only secondarily structural. The outward form, traditions, customs, practices, and policies of the Church that many find so repugnant today spring from a particular theological self-understanding. It is for the purpose of challenging this conventional wisdom that this book has been written.

Such a critique of traditional ecclesiology, with its subsequent attempt at fashioning a newer, more realistic theology of the Church, is not the exclusive concern of Christians and certainly not of interest only to Catholics. The Church is a social, historical, economic, political, and cultural fact of life, writ large. It is heavily endowed financially and continues to exercise an extraordinary amount of intellectual and moral control over an exceedingly large number of people. This latter observation is advanced without prejudice to the clear evidence that the number of Christians who take the institutional Church seriously is decreasing.

The leadership of the Church supports or opposes given legislation, commands or forbids certain practices, com-

mends or discourages particular attitudes and prejudices—
and always in virtue of an implicit theology of the Church.
Ecclesiastical leaders act the way they act (or refuse to act)
because of their ecclesiology, even when it is only implicit
and unreflective. And so it is with the rank-and-file membership. Consequently, how Christians conceive their relationship with the Church and, more fundamentally still, how
they conceive of the nature and mission of the Church in
itself, affects every religious attitude which they have
fashioned, consciously or not. And how Christians conceive
of their Church and its function has immediate pertinence
for the non-Christian and, indeed, even for those who have
no religious affiliation at all.

If the Christian Church were not a social, political, or
cultural force in our society, the outsider could look upon
our theological enterprise as one of the many harmless games
that Christians play. But theology, and more specifically
ecclesiology, comes uncomfortably close to life. Therefore,
while it is of more immediate concern to Christians themselves that an accurate and meaningful theology of the
Church be constructed, an attempt such as this to rethink
the nature and mission of the Christian community in the
world should merit the attention and critical concern of every
person whose life is affected, in one way or another, by the
presence and activity of the Church. This is a group with
considerable numerical strength.

Others in the Roman Catholic tradition have addressed
themselves in recent years to the problem of the Church.
The attention some few of them have attracted far surpasses
the theological sophistication of their arguments. William
DuBay's *The Human Church*[5] and James Kavanaugh's *A
Modern Priest Looks at his Outdated Church*[6] are dramatic
examples of contemporary protest within the Roman Catholic Church. Robert Adolfs' *The Grave of God* operates at

roughly the same level: it is nonprofessional and nonaca-
demic. He, too, is primarily concerned with the world of
structures and appearances, but he is theologically more alert
and he argues his case with commendable restraint.[7]

My book shares these concerns, but there the similarity
ends. This is not an occasional tract nor just another link in
an expanding chain of social protest from within the
Church's clerical body. But I write conscious of the fact
that a theologian's responsibility transcends his immediate
relationship with the theological community itself. This
book is addressed to my professional colleagues, and much
of it is written in criticism of certain of their assumptions
(again, my point of reference shifts to Roman Catholicism).
In a sense, the book is offered as a challenge, not simply to
that admirable minority which is willing to express its ideas
in print, but especially to the larger group which teaches in
our universities, colleges, and seminaries. And it is directed
as well to the many other people, the nonprofessional
theologians (laymen, priests, ministers, and religious), who
are intelligent, literate, critical, and yet still have hope for
the future of the Church.

My thesis is that Christians must be prepared for a Copernican Revolution in their attitude toward the Church. To
this extent, my argument bears some similarity to that of
Bishop John Robinson who proposed, with limited success,
that a parallel revolution must affect our ideas about God.[8]
The Church is no longer to be conceived as the center of
God's plan of salvation. Not all men are called to membership in the Church, nor is such membership a sign of present
salvation or a guarantee of future salvation. The central
reality is not the Church but the Kingdom of God (and the
Kingdom of Christ insofar as he is the embodiment of God's
Kingdom). The Kingdom of God is the reign and rule of
God in Christ, and it comes into being wherever and when-

ever men love one another and accept one another's burdens with a spirit of compassion, concern, generosity, and sensitivity. All men are called to the Kingdom; not all men are called to the Church.

This thesis contradicts the popular idea that the Church is the ordinary means of salvation and that the Church's primary, if not exclusive, task is to grow and multiply and then to consolidate its gains.[9] In this view, the mission of the Church is 'the missions'. The goal of history is that all men should, on the final day, be assembled together into the Body of Christ. In the meantime, the Church must work and struggle without ceasing to bring as many people as possible within her perimeter, and to keep them there by every imaginable policy of appeasement and compromise. To leave the Church is to abandon salvation; to enter the Church is to embrace eternal life.

On the contrary, the Church is but the sign and instrument of the Kingdom of God, the community of those who have been elected by God to give explicit witness to what has happened, is happening, and will happen in history. It is the Kingdom and not the Church which is the ground and goal of all history. It is the Kingdom and not the Church which is the only theological absolute. The Church, however, is that community which alone gives public acknowledgment of its faith in the Lordship of the Risen Christ. The Church's task is to announce to the world that the Kingdom is among us and even now in the process of growth and development. She must spend herself as God's servant and the world's in the realization of the Kingdom here and now. And, finally, she must demonstrate the meaning and value of the Kingdom by the quality and character of her own life as a community. She must be, in a real sense, the preview of coming attractions, the first fruits of the final and perfect Kingdom, a model city and the pattern according to which men work to build the human community itself. The function of the Church, therefore, is *kerygmatic, diakonic,* and *koinoniac.* She must be both the sign of the Kingdom and the instrument of its realization in history. Her total mission is best expressed by the ecclesial title, Servant Church, for she is the very Body of the Suffering Servant of God, the one who was raised up only after his humiliation and suffering service (Phil 2:5–11), the one who came 'not to be served, but to serve' (Mk 10:45).

If the Church's task is seen in relationship to the Kingdom of God and, indeed, as subordinate to the Kingdom, then it is evident that the Church's style of life and structural complexion must be flexible and fluid. Accordingly, Christians will be summoned eventually and quite logically not only to a Copernican Revolution but also to an Einsteinian Revolution, to a time of relativity and constant change.[10] The tragedy is that the latter is already in process, and without a prior understanding and acceptance of the former revolution, the Christian is simply incapable of assimilating and grasping the meaning of rapid change within the Church. This book is written, therefore, with this added sense of urgency: that Christians may understand theologically the nature and mission of the Church so that they can accept psychologically, intellectually, and spiritually the radical changes that will inevitably occur at a progressively accelerated pace.

This book proceeds through an introductory comment on the mood of contemporary theology (thereby setting the question of the Church in its proper context) and on to an historical examination of the reality of the Church (the Church of the New Testament and the postbiblical Church, up to and including Pope Pius XII's *Mystici Corporis*). A third Part analyzes the theology of the Church in the documents of the Second Vatican Council, and the final Part, which is the heart of the book, sketches a theology of the Church which, while in continuity with the earlier historical development (including Vatican II), goes far beyond it. Having outlined a theology of Christian secularity in the spirit of the writings of Bonhoeffer, Cox, Robinson, the death-of-God theologians, Gogarten, Moltmann, Rahner, Chardin, Schillebeeckx, Metz, and others, I then apply this theological perspective to such concrete issues as the ecumenical movement, the problem of authority in the Church; the relationship between Christianity and secular humanism and between Catholic Christianity and various non-Catholic expressions of Christianity; conscience, revelation, apologetics, diocesan and parochial structures, the place of the episcopate and the ordained priesthood, intercommunion, and conversion and 'reversion' (the Charles Davis case, for example).[11]

The book is directed toward all Christians (although the key references to Vatican II may seem to make it of more immediate concern to Catholics), and it should also be of interest to non-Christians, for whom fundamental changes within the Christian community have at least indirect import. From a Catholic point of view, it is designed not only to provide a commentary and analysis of the theology of Vatican II, but also to explore the council's antecedents and, in particular, the implications and consequences of the council's concept of the Church. In the end, the book does not accept uncritically the council's notion of the Church and, in fact, suggests that much of its ecclesiology is inadequate for our time. In a word, the Second Vatican Council stopped short at raising and answering the most radical ecclesiological question: why should there be a Church at all?

Part One

THE
SECULAR MOOD OF
CONTEMPORARY
THEOLOGY

Chapter 1

The Secular Meaning
of the Gospel

The principal questions in contemporary Christian theology are secular in character. How can the postbiblical, postmedieval Christian continue to make sense of his faith in the light of his own present experience (the secular meaning of the Gospel)? If, indeed, the world has 'come of age' through the twin processes of industrialization and urbanization, then what is to be the specific place and function of the Christian community (the secular mission of the Church)? Some qualifications are in order.

What is Theology?

In the classic meaning of the term, theology is 'faith seeking understanding' (St Anselm). Theology is the scientific and systematic reflection of the Church upon her faith. Its chief aim is understanding, not certitude. Theology is there to give us a greater understanding of what we already believe. Apart from faith, theology has no meaning. It is subordinate to faith and remains under the control of faith. Theology is, in a real sense, a 'paradoxical enterprise' (Charles Davis). Thinking and believing, reason and faith, are not born to harmony. Their reconciliation is achieved only with effort.

Consequently, theology must be methodical and scientific. It must be prepared to examine each aspect of the Christian faith in the light of its own historical development. That is, theology must always have its starting point in Sacred Scripture, in the writings of the Fathers of the Church, in the official teachings of the councils, and so forth. Theological understanding will grow also when elements of the faith are viewed in relation to other elements. Thus, a more profound understanding of the person and work of Christ will enlighten our understanding of the nature and mission of the Church, which is his Body. The ultimate goal of theology as an intellectual discipline is the translation of acquired understanding into 'the clearest and most coherent language available'.[1] Theology, therefore, aims at verbal expression with the corresponding demand that such expression be intelligible and consistent. Theological statements must possess not only an internal consistency but also a coherence with all the other intellectual enterprises. That is, theology must hang together from within, and fit together from without.

The Principal Questions in Contemporary Christian Theology

Accordingly, theology must be the servant of faith and of the entire Christian community, which is the Church. It best serves this community when it assists the Church in sorting out and making sense of its commitment to the Gospel and when it indicates the implications of this Gospel faith in time and history. Theology must be Barthian insofar as it should provide an adequate understanding of the content of the Gospel itself, and it must be Tillichian insofar as it seeks to correlate the Gospel message with the situation as it really exists. Thus, if a particular kind of theology is meaningless to the individual believer or irrelevant to the real needs of the Church, then this theology is failing in its essential task. The same Karl Barth has written:

Is there not also an astonishing disparity between what is important, discussed, and more or less victoriously put in action in theology, and the errors and confusions, the sea of suffering and misery prevailing in the world that surrounds theology? . . . *There*, amidst the world, is the still 'unconquered past' of the madness of dictators. . . . There are the murderers and the murdered of the concentration camps. There are Hiroshima, Korea, Algeria, and the Congo. There is the undernourishment of the greater part of mankind. There is the cold war and the sinister threat of a 'hot' one, which might very well be the last. In other words, there is the stubbornly promoted end of all life on our planet.

Here, however, in the realm of theology [Barth continues] is a little de-mythologizing in Marburg and a little *Church Dogmatics* in Basel. *Here* are the rediscovery of the 'historical' Jesus and the glorious new discovery of a 'God above God.' *Here* are the discussions on Baptism and the Eucharist, Law and Gospel, Kerygma and myth, Romans 13 and the heritage of Dietrich Bonhoeffer. *Here* are ecumenical discussions and Church councils. . . . But Kyrie Eleison!—what is the real relationship to everything that simultaneously happened *there*?[2]

Although Barth's purposes were slightly different from my own, the challenge of theological relevancy can be dramatized by paraphrasing Barth's lines and giving them an application that is at once more American and more contemporary: Is there not an astonishing disparity between what some theologians regard as important, what they discuss and write about, and the actual situation in the world today? And is there not an equally astonishing disparity between what interests some members of the Church in this same area of theology, and the actual situation in the world around them?

There we are faced with a senseless armaments race, a race that no nation can win—a race, indeed, in which there can be only disaster for all sides (see the Council's *Pastoral Constitution on the Church in the Modern World*, art. 81). *There* we are confronted with a morally ambiguous war in southeast Asia, where neither side can absolve itself of cruelty and inhumanity and from which a major world war could yet develop. *There* is the problem of poverty and illiteracy, of subhuman housing conditions, inadequate educational facilities, drug addiction, and mental illness (see the same *Pastoral Constitution*, art. 88). *There* we find civil injustice and racial turmoil, bitter and violent, and born of frustration arising from the conditions enumerated above (see the Council's *Declaration on the Relationship of the Church to non-Christian Religions*, art. 5).

And what do we find *here*—here in the world of theology? *Here* we have some discussion on the relationship between Scripture and Tradition: are there two sources of revelation or only one? *Here* we can examine the tempest over transubstantiation, transignification, and transfinalization in the Eucharist. *Here* we read heated essays on clerical celibacy and the problem of authority and obedience in the Church. *Here* we speak of 'the Word' and 'salvation history' and 'the Omega Point'.

This is not meant to suggest that whatever lacks immediate and direct reference to world problems must be discounted as being of no consequence for the faith and mission of the Church. To make such a suggestion would be to set the Church once again on an anti-intellectual course, and she has never gone down that path without the gravest of consequences. The point of these remarks has been to underline the essential connection between the work of theology and the life of the Church in the world. A theology which takes no notice of that connection has forfeited its right to be read or listened to. Accordingly, the *principal* questions in contemporary Christian theology are secular in character because they bring the thinking and reflection of the Church to that jagged edge where Christian faith must grapple with the swiftest currents of the age.

The Meaning of 'Secularity'

It should not be necessary at this relatively late stage to insist that 'secular' does not mean 'secularist'. Following C. A. van Peursen and Friedrich Gogarten, Harvey Cox defines secularization as 'the liberation of man from religious and metaphysical tutelage, the turning of his attention away from other worlds and toward this one.'[3] For the Catholic theologian Johannes Metz, secularization is a process by which modern man, no longer experiencing the world as an imposed fate or as a sovereign sacrosanct nature confining him, 'not only alters the world and forms it into the stage props for his own historical drama, but he also dominates the world through technology.'[4]

Metz's orientation is very much in the spirit (and indeed the letter) of the theology of Jürgen Moltmann[5] who, in turn, has been influenced by the Marxist philosopher Ernst Bloch.[6] Metz has argued against the prevailing theology of recent years, which has been a theology of transcendental, existential, and personalist orientation. This has produced an unhealthy concentration on the individual, private sphere of life. Indeed, theology itself has been 'privatized'. The Gospel was taken merely as a word addressed to the person, as God's personal self-communication, and not as a promise given to men and to society. A contemporary theologian who must bear primary responsibility for this development is Rudolf Bultmann, whose existential interpretation of the New Testament proceeds within the closed circuit of this I-Thou relationship. And Bultmann, in turn, has been a disciple of Martin Heidegger.

Accordingly, we may pause to speculate, as Harvey Cox has done, 'on how different theology would be today if Ernst Bloch, rather than Martin Heidegger, had been our conversation partner for the past twenty years. Would we be as miserably lacking as we are in a theologically grounded social ethic? Would we be as disastrously out of touch with the revolution that is transforming the third world and burning the centers of our American cities? Would we have needed the catharsis of the death-of-God theology? Would we have allowed the ecclesiastical furniture shuffling of recent years to pose as a real renewal of the Church? Might we have produced a theology that was truly radical in its impact on the world and not in its rhetoric?'[7]

On the other hand, John C. Bennett has offered a moderate critique of the new secular theology in his essay, 'The Church and the Secular'.[8] Bennett insists upon a distinction between the 'normative' secular, which has a wholly positive meaning, and the 'prevailing culture'. By the former he means 'freedom from tribalisms, from obsessive ideologies, from the prejudices that are so familiar in our own society, from secularism as a system. It means a healthy pluralism that knows neither old nor new forms of spiritual bondage. It means also freedom from religion, but the catch is that here the secular is interpreted as open in a special way to the biblical revelation (which, by definition, is not religious).

In other words, faith in Christ has a privileged position in the truly secular order that has won freedom from "religion".' The secular, insofar as it applies to the prevailing culture, consists of all the forces and powers which work against the Gospel and the Kingdom of God: 'the effort to maintain white supremacy or white exclusiveness, our anti-Communist obsession, the disproportionate trust in military power, the rat race that leads to economic success, the reductionist view of life that has no more place for what these thinkers associate with Christ than it has for what is called "religion".'[9]

Bennett's fundamental criticism of Cox and the other celebrants of secularity is that they fail to make this distinction clear, with the result that there is a real danger of compromising the prophetic and judgmental role of the Church in society. While this may be the inherent temptation of any secular theologian, I do not think that the criticism applies to Cox, or to Metz, or to any of the other major theologians discussed in this book. Furthermore, it should be clear that there is no essential opposition between Bennett's understanding of secularity and that of the secularizers themselves.

Secular Christianity is not a Christianity without God, or Christ, or the Church, or worship, or the sacraments, or prayer. But it does mean leaving behind the narrow concept by which religion is often understood in our time. This is the notion that religion is purely otherworldly, that it has nothing ultimately to do with the concerns of this world, that it is simply a matter of individual taste and preference, that it is preoccupied only with the sphere of private morality and ethics, that it has no place in the social, political, or cultural areas of life. Indeed, the Second Vatican Council has characterized this dichotomized view of the Gospel as being 'among the more serious errors of our age'.[10] A secular orientation means, rather, that the Gospel comes uncomfortably close to life. It is addressed to this world and is meant to be applicable to the needs of this world.[11]

The Emergence of Secular Theology

But, of course, Christian theology has not always been secular in orientation, even in this 'orthodox' sense. The twentieth century alone has seen Christian theology proceed through sharp and, at times, abrupt changes and shifts of emphasis. In the earlier part of the century, Protestant theology was dominated by its concern for the social gospel. Liberalism, in accordance with its reductionist posture, presented Jesus as a social reformer and the Kingdom of God as an ideal to be realized within our history. Karl Barth, once an advocate of this position, reacted vehemently against this kind of theology and produced his famous commentary on the Epistle to the Romans that truly changed the course of Protestant theology. The First World War had shattered the Liberal illusion and Barth became the prophet of reconstruction.

Catholic theology entered its own social gospel phase in high gear in the 1930s and 1940s under the impact of the massive changes which affected Catholics so directly (the struggle for labor unionism is a case in point). Pope Pius XI's encyclical, *Quadragesimo Anno*, and the many champions of social justice (in this country, Msgr John A. Ryan serves as a good example) dominated the theological scene. Catholic theology has also passed through (and in many respects, is *still* passing through) its own Barthian stage. Barth had argued for a return to the spirit of the Reformation in all its force and purity, which meant a theology that was at once kerygmatic, Christ-centered, and biblical. For a time the Catholic catechetical program was in the mighty grip of the kerygmatic jargon: salvation history (*Heilsgeschichte*), the marvelous acts of God in history (*mirabilia Dei*), and so forth. Theology suddenly became biblical, and Catholic biblicists suddenly became celebrities. Indeed, Catholicism attempted to drop its scholastic heritage so abruptly, with a certain measure of self-consciousness and embarrassment, that some were even suspicious of any attempt to construct a genuinely systematic, philosophically oriented theology.

After the Second World War, Protestant theology shifted its concern to the Church as such. The ecumenical movement and its correlative concern for Church structures was stimulated as much by the common suffering and deprivation of war as by any dispassionate consideration of theological questions. Protestants became very much engaged with the nature and mission of the Church (particularly the latter), and the growth and development of the World Council of Churches merely dramatizes this shift of emphasis. And that is about where 'radical' Catholic theology stands at the moment. Catholics are now addressing themselves honestly and, in some few instances, almost ruthlessly to the question of the Church. The Second Vatican Council itself was concerned in a direct and concentrated fashion with the ecclesiological problematic. In his address to the bishops at the opening of the second session of the council, Pope Paul VI reviewed the 'main objectives' of Vatican II: 'The knowledge, or . . . the awareness of the Church; its reform; the bringing together of all Christians in unity; the dialogue of the Church with the contemporary world.' The central question for the Second Vatican Council was clearly the question of the Church.

But the council was not nearly radical enough (which is the underlying thesis of this book). It did not really confront the question of the Church's very existence. It did not call into question some of its traditional assumptions: Is the

Church the ordinary means of salvation? Is it the center and goal of all history? Are all men in fact called to membership in this community? What, indeed, is its mission? Contemporary Catholic theology is radical when it is willing to subject even Vatican II to careful, critical scrutiny. In the light of both the biblical and ecumenical movements (both of which affected Catholic theology much later than Protestant theology), Catholic theology is just beginning to examine more carefully and more deeply the central relationship between the Church and the Kingdom of God,[12] and it has begun to reflect meaningfully on the minority status of the Christian community in the world.[13]

Meanwhile Protestant theology has moved ahead once again. Now the radical theologians on the Protestant side are addressing themselves to the ultimate theological issue: the problem of God. The 'death-of-God' theologians dramatized this shift of emphasis, but they were, of course, neither the first to attack the problem nor were they alone in trying to solve it. Catholic theology has yet to make any significant steps into this area, although future Catholic efforts will no doubt proceed in the afterglow of the pioneering work of Teilhard de Chardin. If Leslie Dewart's *Future of Belief* is simplistic or superficial, then it is only symptomatic of the infancy and immaturity of Catholic thought on this central question.[14] But Catholic theology would commit a grievous error if it attempted to leap over the preliminary steps leading into this present debate about God. It is a sign of health and vitality, not sluggishness, that Catholic theology should be raising anew (more accurately, for the first time) the Reformation issues. If Catholic theology is to make any distinctive contribution, its growth must be organic and measured. It should be accustomed by now, and therefore not unduly troubled, by its 'tagalong' relationship with Protestant theology in this century. In some instances, Catholic theologians have learned and profited by Protestant mistakes and have maintained a sense of balance and reserve in the construction of their own theological syntheses. Consequently, Catholic theology must address itself to the question of the Church.

In this first Part or section, I am attempting to place this question of the Church in its proper theological context. I have suggested thus far that it is a secular question, which means that we must first come to some understanding of secularity and to an assessment of its impact on the Christian faith. Subsequent to our recognition and acknowledgment of the process of secularization ('the world come of age'), the question that arises with immediate force is the question of the Church. If, indeed, our understanding of the world and of history is secularized, then how can we continue to make sense of our Christian faith, conceptually localized in scholastic or even biblical categories? And since this faith arises from and is essentially linked with a community of faith, then what is to be the specific place and function of this community in the world and in history? What follows in this Part is a detailed summary and interpretative survey of the current state of the discussion concerning both these questions.

The attempt to understand the Christian faith in the light of our newly secularized consciousness is, for our purposes here, the prolegomenon to the question of the Church. The two questions are radically inseparable, and this is demonstrated in the recent writings of Bishop John Robinson, who brought both of them to the surface of public interest and attention. *Honest to God* (1963) and *The New Reformation?* (1965) constitute a kind of diptych: the first raises the question of the secular meaning of the Gospel, and the second poses the question of the secular mission of the Church. *Honest to God* urges a radical recasting of our most fundamental theological categories (God, the supernatural, and religion itself), and *The New Reformation?* confronts the implications of this recasting for the life and work of the Christian community. Indeed, the key to understanding all of Robinson's thought lies in his emerging doctrine of the Church.[15]

Source of the Discussion: Dietrich Bonhoeffer

Although it would be historically shortsighted and naïve to assume that the tradition behind Robinson's revolution was only twenty years long, it is difficult to exaggerate the importance of Dietrich Bonhoeffer's *Letters and Papers from Prison* as the source and inspiration of the secular mood of contemporary Christian theology. After all, Bonhoeffer himself had been the product of a long and complex theological tradition. Born in 1906, he had been a student of Harnack and Karl Barth. In 1928 and 1929 he was a pastor in Barcelona. The next year he came to New York to the Union Theological Seminary where he began to forge a close relationship with Reinhold Niebuhr. Upon his return to Germany, he taught at Berlin until 1936, when the Nazis forbade him to continue. Earlier (1933–5) he had gone to London in protest against the nationalism of some German churches, so his patriotic credentials were somewhat tarnished in the eyes of the new leaders of the Third Reich. He was called back to Germany to lead an emergency seminary movement and during this general period wrote his *Cost of Discipleship* and *Life Together*. In 1939 he returned to the United States for a lecture tour and was encouraged by his American friends and admirers, Niebuhr included, to remain here until the crisis in Germany had passed. But Bonhoeffer refused to accept any form of exile, convinced that his true responsibilities demanded his return home to participate in the resistance movement. For a time he was given extraordinary freedom of movement, but he was eventually imprisoned on April 5, 1943. From that day until October 8, 1944, he was confined to Tegel Prison in Berlin. The letters in the first part of his *Letters and Papers from Prison* were addressed to his parents and were designed especially to allay their fears and anxiety about him. These letters were initially censored, but when he made friends with the guards and medical orderlies, he was able to avoid much of this censorship and hence the quality of the letters improved.

On July 20, 1944, the plot to kill Hitler failed. Bonhoeffer was later linked with that plot and in September the Gestapo removed him to Prinz Albert Strasse. Whatever letters he wrote from here have been lost. Subsequently he moved to Buchenwald, Schönberg, and finally to Flossenburg. On April 8, 1945, he was hanged.

This brief sketch of Bonhoeffer's life and career is sufficient to suggest that the theology of the secular (both the secular meaning of the Gospel and the secular mission of the Church) which he developed during his prison days was a theology forged on the anvil of genuine experience. He could have had no sense of easy optimism, for his celebration of the secular was constructed from within the context of international disaster.

In his letter of April 30, 1944, Bonhoeffer raised the question of the secular meaning of the Gospel: '. . . what *is* Christianity, and indeed what *is* Christ, for us today? The time when men would be told everything by means of words, whether theological or simply pious, is over, and so is the time of inwardness and conscience, which is to say the time of religion as such. We are proceeding towards a time of no religion at all: men as they are now simply cannot be religious any more.'[16] How can Christ become the Lord even of those with no religion?

And then Bonhoeffer immediately introduced the correlative question of the Church. After acknowledging Karl Barth's contribution in being among the first to raise the question of religion-and-Gospel and to delineate clearly the one from the other, Bonhoeffer criticizes his former teacher's positivism of revelation.[17] For Karl Barth, the Gospel comes to modern man on a take-it-or-leave-it basis. This is nothing more than a restoration of biblicism and Reformation orthodoxy. Modern man is asking how he can continue to be a Christian in the light of his own contemporary secular experience. And so Bonhoeffer raises the second question: 'What is the significance of a Church (church, parish, preaching, Christian life) in a religionless world? . . . In what way are we in a religionless and secular sense Christians, in what way are we the *Ekklesia*, "those who are called forth", not conceiving of ourselves religiously as specially favored, but as wholly belonging to the world?'

For Bonhoeffer the problem of God is an aspect of the problem of secularity. In a world come of age, 'God becomes superfluous as a *deus ex machina*.' 'I should like to speak of God,' he wrote, 'not on the borders of life but at its center, not in weakness but in strength, not, therefore, in man's suffering and death but in his life and prosperity. . . . The "beyond" of God is not the beyond of our perceptive faculties. . . . God is the "beyond" in the midst of our life.' And again, the inevitable connection with the problem of the Church: 'The Church stands not where human powers give out, on the borders, but in the center of the village.'

Bonhoeffer criticizes the traditional Christian apologetic as an attack upon the adulthood of the world. 'Efforts are made to prove to a world thus come of age that it cannot live without the tutelage of "God" ' (June 8, 1944). This apologetic is pointless, ignoble, and un-Christian. It is pointless because it is really an attempt to put an adult back into adolescence, making him dependent again upon things which he is no longer dependent upon and thrusting him back into the midst of problems which are no longer problems for him. The traditional Christian apologetic is ignoble because it is an exploitation of the weakness of man for purposes alien to him and not freely subscribed to by him. And it is un-Christian because it seeks to substitute human law, i.e., the religiousness of man, for Christ (June 8, 1944).

The traditional Christian apologetic assumes that salvation means a liberation from this world and the entrance into another world, up there and out there. Damnation comes to those who take this world too seriously and who thereby ignore the realities and the demands of the next. Salvation is the reward for those who endure the hardships and difficulties and setbacks of this life. But 'the Christian, unlike the devotees of the salvation myths, does not need a last refuge in the eternal from earthly tasks and difficulties. But like Christ himself ("My God, my God, why hast thou forsaken me?") he must drink the earthly cup to the lees, and only in his doing that is the crucified and risen Lord with him, and he crucified and risen with Christ. This world must not be prematurely written off . . . Christ takes hold of a man in the center of his life' (June 27, 1944).

The only way the Christian can be honest is to recognize that we have to live in the world *etsi deus non daretur* (July 16, 1944). 'God is teaching us that we must live as men who can get along very well without him. . . . Before God and with him we live without God. God allows himself to be edged out of the world and on to the cross. God is weak and powerless in the world, and that is exactly the way, the only way, in which he can be with us and help us' (July 16, 1944). For Bonhoeffer this is the decisive difference between

Christianity and every other religion. The conventional religious posture is to dwell upon man's weakness and to look upon God as the solution to his distress. God becomes, in this instance, a *deus ex machina*. But the Christian faith in its primitive biblical expression directs man to the powerlessness and suffering of God. Indeed, 'only a suffering God can help.'[18]

'To this extent,' Bonhoeffer concludes, 'we may say that the process we have described by which the world came of age was an abandonment of a false conception of God, and a clearing of the decks for the God of the Bible, who conquers power and space in this world by his weakness. This must be the starting point for our "worldly" interpretation' (July 16, 1944). The Christian, therefore, is the one who willingly and knowlingly participates in the sufferings of God at the hands of a godless world. 'To be a Christian does not mean to be religious in a particular way . . . but to be a man' (July 18, 1944). 'The Christian is not a *homo religiosus*, but a man, pure and simple, just as Jesus was a man' (July 18, 1944).

Accordingly, for Bonhoeffer, worldliness or secularity means 'taking life in one's stride, with all its duties and problems, its successes and its failures, its experiences and helplessness' (July 18, 1944). But his concept of secularity is neither naïve nor purely humanistic. It is a position formulated in the confinement of prison and upon the radical conviction that 'the truth is that if this earth was good enough for the Man Jesus Christ, if a man like him really lived in it, then, and only then, has life a meaning for us. If Jesus had not lived, then our life, in spite of all the other people we know and honour and love, would be without meaning' (August 21, 1944).

Christology becomes the link, in Bonhoeffer's thought, between his analysis of the secularization of the world and his call for a re-examination of the mission of the Church in this world come of age. The Christian encounters Jesus as the man for others, and this concern of Jesus for others is the experience of transcendence. 'Our relation to God (is) not a religious relationship to a supreme Being, absolute in power and goodness, which is a spurious conception of transcendence, but a new life for others, through participation in the Being of God' ("Outline for a Book," Chap. 2). God for us is 'man existing for others, and hence the Crucified.'

And so Bonhoeffer reaches the practical conclusion of his entire argument. 'The Church is her true self only when she exists for humanity. . . . She must tell men, whatever their calling, what it means to live in Christ, to exist for others. . . . It is not abstract argument, but concrete example which gives her word emphasis and power' ("Outline for a Book," Chap. 3). Instead, the Church has spent most of its time and energy in a program of self-preservation, with a corresponding unwillingness to take risks in the service of humanity. Just as Jesus is uniquely the Suffering Servant of God, so, too, must the Church continue this mission.

People who read Dietrich Bonhoeffer's other works before they have confronted his *Letters and Papers from Prison* are oftentimes mystified by the Bonhoeffer cult. They find it almost impossible to share the profound enthusiasm which so many of his latter-day disciples seem to manifest. Bonhoeffer comes through in his earlier works (*The Cost of Discipleship, Life Together*, etc.) as an essentially conservative, evangelical theologian. How explain the extraordinarily diversified influence he has had in contemporary Christian theology?[20] It should also be pointed out that this same sense of bafflement engulfs even those who begin to dip into the *Letters and Papers from Prison*. Throughout the first half of the book Bonhoeffer comes across as perhaps an unusually sensitive man, gifted with a kind of poetic expression, whose primary concern in prison is to allay the anxieties of his

parents and friends about the state of his health. The reader
should not be put off by these introductory pages. These
letters were written when censorship was still being rigor-
ously imposed and during the period when Bonhoeffer
was understandably concerned about his parents' reaction to
his plight. However, we have in the latter half of the book
and particularly in the last third of the *Letters* the ideas
which 'split rocks' (to use Bishop Robinson's description) in
twentieth-century Christian theology.

An historian of theology need not apologize for any
excessive interest in the work of Bonhoeffer. His influence is
an undeniable fact and the multiple character of this influence
is equally beyond question. The Bonhoeffer spirit is evident
in the later writings of the Anglican Bishop Robinson, the
Baptist Harvey Cox, the three 'death-of-God' theologians,
Thomas J. J. Altizer, William Hamilton, and Paul van
Buren, the German Catholic Johannes B. Metz, the Catholic
philosopher Leslie Dewart, and others. The enumeration of
these names alone gives some indication of the kind of influence Bonhoeffer has had, for these theologians represent
a rather wide expanse on the contemporary theological
spectrum. The observation of Martin Marty, an unusually
perceptive theological reporter and Church historian, merits
repetition here: 'Younger European and American Christian
thinkers often seem to be divided into two camps: those who
acknowledge their debt to Bonhoeffer and those who are
indebted but who obscure the traces to their source.'[21]

The Deprofessionalization of the Discussion: Bishop Robinson

Bishop John A. T. Robinson's place in the history of
twentieth-century theology is secure, but it is not for any
of his scholarly writings in the field of New Testament

studies or for any of his pastoral achievements in the suffragan diocese of Woolwich in south London. Robinson's principal contribution to Christian theology has been, ironically, one of his least theological efforts. *Honest to God*, published in March of 1963, is a veritable watershed in modern Church history, occupying a place alongside of Karl Barth's commentary on *Romans*. In this regard, Robinson's contribution is much like Bonhoeffer's. It was not one of Bonhoeffer's earlier, more academic books (such as *Communio Sanctorum* or *Act and Being*) that sent shock waves through the theological community, but the chance collection of *Letters and Papers from Prison*. And neither *Honest to God* nor Bonhoeffer's *Letters* were given birth in the rarified atmosphere of the groves of academe. Both were produced within the context of unvarnished reality: Robinson facing the overwhelming irrelevance of Christianity in England, Bonhoeffer confronting national madness and personal destruction.

Professional theologians of every persuasion found time to scoff at the naïveté or gross superficiality of *Honest to God*. Many complained of Robinson's careless lumping of Bultmann, Tillich, and Bonhoeffer into a single glob of theological dough. Even his most sympathetic critics wondered aloud about the organization and coherence of the argumentation. But none of these critics could deny that Robinson had accomplished what no other professional theologian had been able to achieve. Robinson alone had been able to bring these genuinely contemporary issues to the surface of public interest and attention. It was Robinson, not Bultmann, who alerted the general populace to the issues of myth and message; it was Robinson, not Tillich, who raised questions about our whole supernaturalistic framework; and it was Robinson, and none of these other professional theologians, who brought the insights of Dietrich Bonhoeffer to the larger community of literate, intelligent, critical—but non-professional—students of theological issues. What was it that surfaced with Robinson's depth charge?

Three central theological debates came into view: the discussion about God, the reexamination of the place of Christ, and the question of the Church and the Christian life. What issues could be of more burning concern to Christian theology than these?

Robinson suggested that much of the disorder in our thinking about the Church and the Christian life must be laid at the doorstep of a primitive concept of God and a mythological notion of Jesus Christ. And so his *Honest to God* is structured along these lines, addressing itself in turn to the problems of supranaturalism, mythology, and religiosity.[22]

According to Robinson, supranaturalism is 'a way of thinking in which God is posited as the highest Being—out there, existing over and beyond this world . . . alongside and over and above his creation' (p. 30). With Bonhoeffer, he takes his stand firmly against every notion which reduces God to a *deus ex machina*, a problem-solver of sorts (see p. 47). Following Paul Tillich he suggests that God is the unconditional who is found with and under the conditional relationships of life (see pp. 52–53 and 60), and that God is not met by a turning away from this world but in an unconditional concern for 'the other' (p. 61).

The way into an encounter with ultimacy is Christ. And so Robinson raises the second of his questions: Must Christianity be mythological? Traditional Christology is frankly supranaturalistic in Robinson's view (and here he is drawing upon Rudolf Bultmann). Much of Christian spirituality and preaching is frankly docetic (p. 64). Christ is conceived as God dressed up as a human person, God in human form. Docetism historically refuses to grant full humanity to Jesus of Nazareth. There is something inherently evil about the world of matter. Total incarnation is unthinkable. But the paradox is that Jesus never made any personal claims. His concern was always for the Father, that the Kingdom of God might be established and realized throughout all of creation (p. 73). Jesus is *homoousios*, of one substance, with the Father because he is completely united to the ground of Being. The essence of Being is love, for as St John insisted: God *is* love. And love is essentially this living for the other, the absence of selfish concern. In Jesus of Nazareth we find no trace of self-centeredness or lack of compassion and sensitivity. He is a man totally oriented to the needs of others. He is uniquely, in Bonhoeffer's phrase (taken over from Karl Barth), 'the man for others' (see p. 76).

If Jesus Christ is our way into the ultimacy of God, what is the way into the embodiment of this love in Christ? At this point, Robinson proposes the third and final problematic: Must Christianity be religious? Herein, the influence of Bonhoeffer is most decisively present, but it is not exclusively here. The spirit of Bonhoeffer's openness to secular reality permeates the whole of Robinson's thinking. The idea of God as the unconditional in the conditional relationships of life may be Tillichian in form but it is Bonhoefferian in spirit. And the concern for the demythologization of Christ from the docetic image of God in human form to the Jesus of the New Testament, the man for others, may be Bultmannian in immediate origin but it is, again, clearly the spirit of Bonhoeffer's celebration of the secular that sustains Robinson's Christology and provides the principal thrust to his argument.

Christianity is religious when it is metaphysical and individualistic. The religious is the antithesis of the secular. It creates problems where there are none; it exposes weaknesses which no longer exist. Accordingly, the Christian must enter the lists against the perennial temptation of religiosity and create a genuinely 'worldly holiness' in liturgy, in prayer, in every area of morality.[23] 'For Christianity . . . the holy is the "depth" of the common, just as the "secular" is not a (godless) section of life but the world (God's world, for which Christ died) cut off and alienated from its true depth' (p. 87). Thus, the function of worship is to 'make us more sensitive to these depths . . . to "the beyond in our midst", to the Christ in the hungry, the naked, the homeless and the prisoner' (pp. 87 and 90). And prayer means opening 'oneself to another *unconditionally* in love' (p. 99). 'Prayer is the responsibility to meet others with *all* I have, to be ready to encounter the unconditional in the conditional, to expect to meet God in the way, not to turn aside from the way' (p. 100). And morality measures the response of the Christian to the call of Jesus, but his teachings are not legislation laying down what love always demands of everyone: 'they are illustrations of what love may at any moment require of anyone' (pp. 110–11). The task of the Christian in our time is 'to join those on the Emmaus road who have no religion left, and there, in, with and under the meeting of man with man and the breaking of our common bread, to encounter the unconditional as the Christ of our lives' (p. 121). And so Robinson comes to the heart of his concern, the secular mission of the Church, which will occupy us in Chapter 2.

The Americanization of the Discussion: Harvey Cox and the 'Death-of-God' Theologians

Harvey Cox: The Secular City

American theology has been, until very recently, a mere echo-chamber for European religious thought. This is still the case, for all practical purposes, in Catholic theology.

But American Protestant theology has begun to do something about this excessive dependence upon European thought. The new series edited by John B. Cobb and James M. Robinson, *New Frontiers in Theology*, has provided some basis for a *mutually* fruitful exchange between American and Continental (particularly German) theologians.[24] There is, however, one area of theological investigation which seems to have acquired a distinctively American character, and that is the discussion of secularization.[25] Although this issue does not lack European voices (Friedrich Gogarten, Bonhoeffer, and Metz are cases in point), it has been the Americans who have brought the matter to the surface and have given it a sense of immediacy and relevance. The United States clearly provides an apt theological laboratory in which to test the implications of a theology of secularity. Indeed, Bonhoeffer's contribution to Christian theology is not readily apparent until the peculiarly American implications of his thought have been developed. And for this spelling out of Bonhoeffer's theses, Christian theology is indebted to the work of Harvey Cox.

'Secularization is man turning his attention away from worlds beyond and toward this world and this time' (*Secular City*, p. 2). Cox's basic premise is identical with Bonhoeffer's, that secularization means 'man's coming of age', but he confesses that this is a tardy theological interpretation of a process that had already been noticed by poets and novelists, sociologists and philosophers, for decades. If secularization designates the content of man's coming of age, then urbanization describes the context in which it is occurring. By urbanization he means 'a structure of common life in which diversity and the disintegration of tradition are paramount' (p. 4).

With Gogarten, Cox argues that secularization is 'the legitimate consequence of the impact of biblical faith on history' (p. 17). He is suggesting here that secularization is not only assimilable into the Christian theological scheme of things but is, in fact, demanded and produced by biblical faith. The creation event reveals the disenchantment of nature; the desacralization of politics is accomplished in the Exodus; and the Sinai Covenant's prohibition of idols gave rise to the deconsecration of values.

With creation, history emerges as the locus of God's action. God and man are separated from nature, which is shorn of all magical aura. Nothing in nature is worthy of adoration or reverential fear, because God and nature are distinct. Nature, therefore, is not something preordained by God, something to be accepted as a given reality. Nature is the raw material for human initiative and innovation. Neither God nor man are defined by their relationship to nature, which means that both God and man are freed for history and that nature is now available for man's own use. This disenchantment of the natural world is an absolute precondition for the development of natural science and it is one of the essential components of secularization.

There can be no significant political or social changes in a society where the rulers and the institutional structures are accorded divine legitimation. The Exodus event teaches that politics is not sacred, that no one man or group of men, and no single institution or larger institutional structure, participate in the prerogatives of divinity. The deliverance from Egypt was an event of social change, a massive act of 'civil disobedience', an act of insurrection against the lawfully constituted authority of the Pharaoh. And yet it became the central event around which the Israelites organized their whole perception of reality. And so it is with solid biblical foundation that Dietrich Bonhoeffer was able to argue for a kind of 'holy worldliness'. The Christian rejects the false cults which counsel an escapist attitude toward the world, but he also rejects the cult of the emperor because, although worldly, it is not holy enough. Jesus alone is Lord.

Finally, the Sinai Covenant provided a certain degree of healthy relativism. This relativization of human values is one of the integral dimensions of secularization and has its roots, partially at least, in the biblical prohibition against graven images. Any deity which could be expressed in the form of an idol was *ipso facto* not Yahweh. The task of the Christian is to foster this process of secularization, prevent it from becoming an ideology (such as secularism itself), and clarify its relationship as often as possible with biblical faith.

Cox's vision is peculiarly American as he delineates the shape and style of the secular city. The social shape of the secular city is characterized by anonymity and mobility, and these are suggested by the images of the switchboard and the cloverleaf. The switchboard is a reminder of the vast network and impersonal structure that constitutes the modern urban complex. The anonymity which the city affords (and which the switchboard typifies) is a liberating phenomenon because it opens up the possibility of freedom in contrast to the bondage of law and convention. Cox does not share the indignation of certain contemporary Christian figures, including some theologians, about the depersonalization of modern urban life. He warns against confusing a preurban ethos with the Christian concept of *koinonia*. The two are not the same. What needs to be developed in our time is a theology of anonymity, a theology of the I-You rather than I-Thou relationship.

The cloverleaf serves as a graphic image of the second characteristic of the secular city: mobility. Other images might serve the purpose equally well: the airport control tower, high-speed elevators, perpetually moving escalators and so forth. High mobility plays havoc with traditional religion, as it separates men from their holy places. It mixes them with neighbors whose gods have different names. Once again, the Bible offers support for the value of mobility. The Israelites were originally a nomadic and essentially homeless people. Their God was a mobile deity, unlike the Baalim of Canaan who were immobilized in particular towns and places. The Baalim were the gods of a sedentary people; Yahweh was the god of men on the move. He always went before them calling them ahead to new frontiers. The Ark of the Covenant dramatizes this fact most effectively. And when the Ark was captured by the Philistines, the Israelites were made to realize that Yahweh was not contained even there. The destruction of the Temple and the loss of their homeland deepened the Jewish understanding of their God. Yahweh could not be localized anywhere, and Jesus built his Gospel upon this developing tradition.

The style of the secular city is pragmatic and profane. President Kennedy stands as an example of the former characteristic, and Albert Camus as example of the latter. If we are to find a nonreligious or secular meaning of the Gospel, as Bonhoeffer insisted, then the qualities of the shape and style of the secular city must inform the understanding and presentation of the message. The pragmatic man does not ask religious questions because he believes that he can handle this world without them. 'Authentic secularity demands that no world-view, no tradition, no ideology be allowed to become the officially enforced world-view beside which no others are tolerated' (*Secular City*, p. 69).

The man for whom secularity is the prevailing spirit knows that the world does not come to him already finished and ordered. It is something to be molded and shaped. Man has been given dominion over it (Gen 1:28), and, in partnership with God, he can recreate it into a theater of human dignity and the highest values of the spirit.

At the beginning of his fifth chapter, Cox insists: 'The

starting point for any theology of the church today must be a theology of social change' (p. 105). The summary thus far provides some indication of the kind of pre-Church theology he would write. 'Our preaching today is powerless,' he concludes, 'because it does not confront people with the new reality which has occurred and because the summons is issued in general rather than in specific terms' (p. 122).[26]

'Death-of-God' Theology

The 'death-of-God' controversy in America preoccupied Christian theology for about a year and a half (1965–6). From the very start it was a nebulous and ambivalent phenomenon, and the situation never really improved. There were times, in fact, when it was difficult even to determine the identity of the 'death-of-God' theologians and to decide whether or not they really did affirm his death. At various junctures in the discussion, the 'death-of-God' camp was said to include Harvey Cox, Gabriel Vahanian, Bishop John Robinson, as well as the three American theologians who were, indeed, the only members of the group from the outset: Thomas J. J. Altizer, William Hamilton, and Paul van Buren.

The 'death-of-God' movement, such as it was, is already in a state of decomposition. Interest could not have been sustained without the continued publicity and attention afforded by the communications media. This has waned considerably, if not completely. But more significantly, the triumvirate itself seems to have folded its tent and slipped silently away. William Hamilton's recent essay in *The Christian Century* ('A Funny Thing Happened on the Way to the Library,' April 12, 1967) seems to contain an implicit admission of superficiality and a clear resolution to return to the books. Paul van Buren has since moved considerably away from his earlier position and seems disenchanted with his former associates for their alleged sensationalizing of a complex and sensitive theological problem.

Much of the comment about 'death-of-God' theology had centered its attention on the theological or doctrinal aspects of the movement. Is God dead or isn't he? In what sense is he dead? How can we rethink the reality of God in the light of modern philosophy and the present course of cultural history? Some theologians were pleased, no doubt, that the attention of the Church had been redirected once again to the central and fundamental question of God's existence, or that the 'death-of-God' stir was challenging Christian theologians to adopt a more theoretical posture (as opposed to what might be described as a 'creeping biblicism'). But others, who have been more concerned with the impact and effectiveness of the Church's mission in the world, were annoyed by the introduction of another 'religious' question, which was diversionary in character because it came at the moment when the Church was preparing, at long last, to move out and to assume her responsibilities in and for the secular city.

But, as a matter of fact, the primary concern of the 'death-of-God' theologians was not doctrinal, but ethical. And their theological point of reference was not God (dead or alive), but Christ as 'the man for others'. To be faithful to the ethical stance of Jesus, to stand at his side in the service of humanity, demands the renunciation of religion and the repudiation of the Church. 'Death-of-God' theology assumed, in other words, that commitment to the world cannot coexist with a commitment to the transcendent Lordship of Christ, and that genuine secularity is an impossible posture for a Christian who continues to take seriously the reality of the Church as the Body of Christ.

For Paul van Buren (see his *Secular Meaning of the Gospel*), all theology must be reduced to Christology (thereby demonstrating some form of influence by his former teacher, Karl Barth). 'God-talk' must be set aside. God, for us, is simply Jesus. And faith in Jesus is essentially an ethical stance. It means living as a 'man for others', living without regard to self, and being caught up in the contagion of Jesus' own freedom. In this view, the Church cannot be called the 'Body of Christ' in a descriptive sense. The theological and biblical designation is merely 'a reference to the historical perspective which the members presumably have in common, and it suggests the harmony that would exist between people who shared this perspective' (p. 184).

William Hamilton's starting point is different from van Buren's (see his *The New Essence of Christianity*[27]), but his orientation and ethical concerns are similar. What has occurred in our time, he argues, is that the biblical portrait of God (and therefore the Reformation portrait of God) has deteriorated to such a point that it is no longer meaningful or acceptable to modern man. The real significance of the Reformation is now becoming clear. It was not primarily a theological or a psychological revolution, but an ethical revolution. The Protestant Reformation meant not so much the discovery of the righteous God (the *theological* dimension) or the victory of the autonomous religious personality (the *psychological* dimension) as the fact that the Church moved from the cloister to the world, toward the world (the *ethical* dimension) and away from religion. We now find ourselves in the position of waiting for God. God has withdrawn, is absent. In the interim period, our obedience is to Jesus. But Jesus is not an object of faith. He is a *place to be*—at the side of the neighbor. And what is the relation of this radical theology to the Church? 'I do not see how preaching, worship, prayer, ordination, the sacraments can be taken seriously,' Hamilton has written. The 'Body of Christ' is irrelevant to the task of secular mission.[28]

Altizer employs a more grandiose intellectual approach to the question of the death of God, although the ethical implications are not sharply or adequately delineated. Employing the dialectical system of Hegel, he suggests that Spirit had to negate itself to become its opposite other, Flesh. The process of negation began with creation and continued with each revelation-event in the Old Testament. The decisive moment occurred at the Incarnation, and specifically on the Cross. At that point, Spirit completely emptied itself and became fully identified with its opposite other. And somehow, at the end of history, there will be a reappearance of Spirit in a new synthesis of Spirit and Flesh. In the meantime, our task is to embrace the profane and the secular, to seek out 'the epiphany of the Word in every human heart and hand'.

According to Altizer's diagnosis, the twentieth century has seen the collapse of the idea of transcendence. The radical Christian must share the agony of modern man and live without God. He must renounce liturgy and doctrine. He must repudiate the sovereign Creator and the transcendent Lord. The Christian must seek, instead, a total union with Jesus, but not with the Jesus of the New Testament. He is beyond recall and is irrelevant, in any case. The manifestation of the Word is 'in every human hand and face'.

In all three instances, the line of thinking proceeds from the abolition of God (understood differently by each of the three men), through the affirmation of Jesus as 'the man for others', and on to the demands of our secular involvement, which is the distinctive ethical dimension.

The first assumption of 'death-of-God' theology, and more specifically of 'death-of-God' ethics, is that the ethical commitment depends upon, and flows organically from, the doctrinal presuppositions: the negation of God and the repudiation of the Church. And secondly, that it is, for all practical purposes, impossible to affirm the values of the secular order without making a declaration of independence from traditional theology: or, inversely, that 'orthodox' Christian theology cannot support an authentic Christian radicalism. I have suggested elsewhere that these assumptions cannot be sustained, theologically or empirically.[29] Since the principal concern of this book is with the question of the Church, I shall defer until Chapter 2 any criticism of the 'death-of-God' ecclesiology. It is sufficient for now to indicate how the original inspiration of Bonhoeffer has been carried into the ambient of American theology and the various possibilities for development that are open to it. The distance between Harvey Cox, on the one hand, and Thomas Altizer, on the other, is considerable—more pronounced, in fact, than many superficial commentators on the contemporary debate about God have been willing to admit or have been able to detect. But all of these theologians *are* united in their concern for the secular order and for making the Gospel meaningful and intelligible for the modern mid-twentieth-century American. An appreciation of this drift of thought in contemporary American theology, and some awareness of its Continental theological roots, seems to me to be essential to any adequate understanding of the whole problem of the Church.

Catholic Participation in the Discussion

Insofar as Catholic theology is traditionally located right of center on the theological spectrum, Catholic theologians have not participated in the initial developments of secular theology. Until very recently, our most progressive theologians were engaged in a sympathetic confrontation with Reformation thought. Catholic theology, by and large, is only now beginning to emerge from its Barthian phase. We should not be surprised or unduly distressed, therefore, that Catholic participation in the dialogue about secularization should be modest, to say the least.

Johannes B. Metz: The European Catholic Response
Although various Catholic theologians have addressed themselves at one time or another, and in one degree or another, to the process of secularization and its implications for a proper understanding of the Gospel, few have given the matter such concentrated attention as Fr. Johannes Metz, a student of Karl Rahner.[30] Father Metz has only recently begun to acquire something of an international reputation. For those Catholics for whom Bonhoeffer and Cox, Gogarten and Robinson, are merely names, Metz's ideas sound strikingly novel and provocative. As a matter of fact, Metz is saying nothing essentially different from those Protestant and Anglican theologians who have already received some attention in this chapter.[31]

Although a student of Rahner, Metz is clearly not satisfied with the modern transcendental, personalistic, and existential theology which places such great stress upon the present moment. This is the theological orientation stimulated by Martin Heidegger (who was Karl Rahner's teacher) and propagated by Rudolf Bultmann. Metz sees this perspective as tending to limit faith by concentrating on the actual moment of the believer's personal decision for Christ and his Gospel. The future is then all but lost.

Secondly, this kind of theology tends to become private and individualistic. It fails to bring into sufficient prominence the social and political implications of the believer's faith and responsibility. Accordingly, Metz proposes three theses which are very much in keeping with our contemporary historical understanding of the world.

First, modern man's understanding of the world is fundamentally oriented toward the future. His mentality, therefore, is not primarily contemplative, but operative. Man no
longer experiences the world as an imposed fate nor as a
sacred order given from above. Rather, it has become the
raw material with which he can build his own new world.
He dominates the world through technology and thereby
secularizes it. What moves man today is not the commitment for the 'world above' but the commitment to build a
new world. In every case, the fundamental orientation is
toward the future, and in this regard Christianity and
Marxism have much in common. (The influence of Moltmann and Ernst Bloch is particularly strong here.)

Metz's second thesis is that the orientation of the modern
era to the future, and the understanding of the world as
history, which results from this orientation, is based upon
the biblical belief in the promises of God. For the Greeks,
history was simply a matter of eternal recurrence. There
is 'nothing new under the sun'. But for the Hebrews, history
is linear and is directed toward the future. The Israelites
were those who were marked by hope, hope in their own
future, hope in the future of history. God revealed himself
to the Israelites not as a God *above* us but as a God *before* us.
He summons us to our common task of building history,
of realizing all the potentialities which have been given to
us.

The proclamation of the resurrection of Jesus in the New
Testament carries forward this same notion of hope and
this same orientation toward the future. We have the 'first
fruits' of the new creation already through the death and
resurrection of the Lord. The Christian mission is to alter
and innovate in the world in order to see that the promises
of God are achieved. For the world is not some static reality.
It is 'arising reality', whose development or process is

committed to the free action of man. This universal altera-
tion and innovation of the world through the offensive of
human freedom characterizes that process which Metz calls
'secularization'. The world (history) is secularized to the
extent that it no longer appears as a fixed and sacrosanct
reality in a preestablished harmony. It is, again, an 'arising
reality', subject to growth and innovation.

Thirdly, this relationship between the Christian faith and
the world should be characterized from a theological point
of view as a creative and militant eschatology. The Christian
is moved to flee and renounce the world not because he
despises the world but because he hopes in the future of the
world as proclaimed in God's promises. The Christian has a
responsibility for the world and for its future.

At this point, Metz suggests an answer to our second
major question: So what for the Church? I shall return to
Metz's position in Chapter 2; here it is sufficient to indicate
the general lines of his ecclesiology. First of all, he insists that
the Church is not the nonworld. Rather, it is that part of the
world which attempts to live from the promised future of
God, and to call that world in question which seeks to live
within its own limited possibilities. The Church, therefore,
is a pilgrim or exodus community. It celebrates the death
and resurrection of Christ, until he comes. The Church is not
the goal of her own activity; this goal is the Kingdom of
God. The Kingdom is even now coming into existence, and
the Church's task is to be its sign and instrument.

And so Christian theology cannot become simply personalistic and existential. It must be a theology of the
emerging political and social order; indeed, it must be a
political theology. For Christian hope is essentially directed
to the world of our brother, since this hope fulfills itself in
love for the other, for the least of our brothers. 'We know
that we have passed out of death into life, because we love

the brethren' (cf. 1 Jn 3:14). Hope is this living for the other. And this, of course, is simply the Gospel. And the realization of the Gospel is the Kingdom of God. This is the goal of all the Church's strivings.

What we have in the writings of Johannes Metz is, in a sense, a 'High-Church' version of Harvey Cox, Friedrich Gogarten, Jürgen Moltmann, and other Protestant celebrants of secularity.

Leslie Dewart: A North American Catholic Response

Leslie Dewart's *Future of Belief: Theism in a World Come of Age*[32] is selected here as a second example of Catholic participation in the discussion about secularization because of the suggestive link he makes between the thought of Dietrich Bonhoeffer and the fundamental orientation of Teilhard de Chardin. Dewart attempts to show, in other words, that the Bonhoeffer tradition has something substantial to gain from a cross-pollination with a distinctly Catholic stream of thought.

Dewart states the problem of the secular meaning of the Gospel very clearly at the beginning of his book: 'the problem of integrating Christian theistic belief with the everyday experience of contemporary man in a modern, industrial, technological society' (p. 7). And he defines contemporary experience as 'the mode of consciousness which mankind, if not as a whole at least in respect of our own civilization constituting man's cultural vanguard, has reached as a result of its historical and evolutionary development' (p. 9). Given this new historical and evolutionary consciousness (disclosed and celebrated by Chardin), 'the integration of theism with today's everyday experience requires not merely the *demythologization of Scripture* but the more comprehensive *dehellenization of dogma*, and specifically that of the Christian doctrine of God' (p. 49).

Dewart, therefore, recognizes that the world has come of
age and that it is a world in which the only meaningful
categories of thought are historical, relational, and evolutionary. Both Dietrich Bonhoeffer and Teilhard de Chardin
recognized this same fact, but from altogether diverse points
of view. Both saw the need for Christian theism to accept
as given the contemporary experience and to feel itself
free to accept novel philosophical foundations. Bonhoeffer
and Teilhard de Chardin can be appropriately paired, despite
the intrinsic weaknesses of each man (see pp. 42–46).

Dewart suggests some of the implications of his argument
in his pivotal third chapter on 'The Development of Christian Dogma'. However, the hypotheses which he weaves in
the final chapter on 'The Development of Christian Theism'
connect his effort more closely and more decisively to the
work of those secular theologians already discussed in this
chapter. 'Since God is wholly present to all of man's and
nature's time,' he argues, 'we should say that this temporality
consists in being *present to history*. The fundamental relation
between man and God is found in the reality of history. It
consists in the mutual presence of God and man in the *conscious* creation of the world' (p. 195). Consequently, all
history is *possible* and all history is *free*. But the unlimited
possibilities and freedom of history can work both ways, for
or against God. History can fail. But it is the unwavering
Christian hope that this real possibility of failure will not in
fact, with God's help, come to pass (see pp. 195–6).

The patent similarities between Dewart's thought and the
views of Cox, Metz, Gogarten, Moltmann, and others are
far greater than the index of Dewart's book would suggest.
What is significant about Dewart's effort, apart now from
his conscious linking of Bonhoeffer with Chardin (an alliance which has yet to be worked out thoroughly at the
professionally theological level), is that it is yet another

independent indication of the secular character of contemporary theological questions. And although he insists at the beginning of his book that he is coming to grips with a theoretical rather than a functional problem, his handling of the problem clearly indicates that the theoretical analysis has immediate functional import. *The Future of Belief* shows, in other words, that the first of our two central questions (how can the mid-twentieth-century Christian continue to make sense of his faith in the light of his own contemporary experience?) leads logically and necessarily into the second, more functional, and more pastorally urgent question: what is to be the mission and place of the Christian community in this world come of age?

Chapter 2

The Secular Mission of the Church

Theological textbooks written prior to the biblical renewal in the Catholic Church described the Church as a visible society founded by Jesus Christ to carry on his work of redemption. Christ has committed to his Church, and specifically to his apostles and their successors, the various means of sanctification and salvation. The Church, therefore, is a perfect society, hierarchically structured, which exists to save people in virtue of the redemptive work of Jesus Christ. Books written after the encyclical letter of Pope Pius XII, *Mystici Corporis* (1943), would add a section on the Church as the Mystical Body of Christ, but this was often interpreted in the same juridical sense.

Ecclesiological studies influenced by the best currents in biblical and patristic scholarship would advance a much more organic concept of the Church. M. J. LeGuillou, O.P., offers such an image of the Church in his recent book, *Christ and Church: A Theology of the Mystery*.[1] He argues that the Church must be seen as a part of God's plan of self-disclosure and his invitation to personal communion with himself. The theme of his study is that Christ is the Word and Wisdom of God manifesting himself in order that he might transform us into his glory. The beginning of this process occurs in the communion of the Church where the transforming revelation of the Mystery is accomplished (see pp. 137 and 219). 'The Church, the Body of Christ, appears as the presence of the Mystery of Christ, and as the organism of its manifestation to the world' (p. 297).

Without question Father LeGuillou's concept of the Church is many strides ahead of the portrait outlined in the earlier manuals of theology. The Church is not simply an organization which has at its disposal the means of salvation and the jurisdictional power to distribute them, but it is uniquely the sacramental presence of the love and mercy of God in history. As the Body of Christ, the Church somehow is the sign and instrument of his presence and the classic point of encounter with him. It is the community of those who have received and acknowledged the Word and Wisdom of God, for the Word itself is formative of community.

The Second Vatican Council adopted this line of thought in developing its own concept of the Church (and we shall return to the council's ecclesiology in Part III). But this newer ecclesiology, more biblical and patristic in inspiration, still labors under several difficulties. In a word, it assumes too much and it leaves unanswered the most radical ecclesiological question of all: Why the Church? It is more concerned with the Church as a community-at-rest, as the Body of Christ, as the mystery of Christ's presence in history, as his sacrament, as the People of God, and so forth. But it leaves aside the burning question of the Church's mission, that is, the functional side of the ecclesiological problematic. For it is not enough to insist that the Church has the Spirit of Christ and that its task is simply to dispense this Spirit as widely as possible. This is a kind of ecclesiastical imperialism, and it is becoming increasingly difficult to accept it without further examination.

The present course of theological thought in this central area of ecclesiology offers hope for some satisfactory answers to the awkward problems of contemporary history. Some theologians (again we are dealing here principally with Protestants and Anglicans, but there are indications of progress in Catholic theology as well) are now asking the question, *Why* the Church? before they are willing to raise the point of the Church's grandeur and destiny as the Body of Christ, People of God, and so forth. What accounts for the change of circumstances? Why have Christian theologians suddenly adopted a more radical posture with regard to the specific place and function of the Christian community in the world and in history? The answer lies in the analysis offered in Chapter 1. The process of secularization has occasioned a profound theological reshuffling in the Church. Everything, as Bishop Robinson suggested in the preface to *Honest to God*, is going into the melting.

Bonhoeffer

Once again, therefore, we can point to Bonhoeffer in order to account for the shift in the ecclesiological winds. It was Bonhoeffer who challenged the Church at its weakest point. For the Church had become in his time, and to a large extent remains in ours, a community which was primarily interested in its own survival and prosperity. And this need not always be a matter of dollars and cents or brick and mortar. For if the Church is seen, in theological terms, as the ordinary means of salvation for all of mankind, then it does assume an inordinate importance in history. All men must be called to membership in the Church; those who enter the Church—by birth or by conversion—must, at every cost, remain within her perimeter. History will have achieved final success when all men are, at last, gathered together in her bosom.

But Bonhoeffer sensed that this theological schema was

completely out of tune with the situation as it really was. The world had come of age and men could not simply accept the Church as the embodiment and custodian of God's Word. How, then, are men to accept the Gospel in terms which make some sense to them?

Bonhoeffer argued that the Church must be like Christ. Jesus came not to be served, but to serve. He is uniquely 'the man for others', the one to whom men must look if they are to unlock the mystery of human life and of all history. Just as Christ is the Suffering Servant of God, so, too, must the Church be a community for others, a servant Church willing to take risks in the service of humanity and willing to provide this service even in the nonreligious categories of contemporary society. 'The Church is her true self only when she exists for humanity. . . . She must tell men, whatever their calling, what it means to live in Christ, to exist for others.'[2]

Robinson

It was in the spirit of Bonhoeffer's vision that Bishop John Robinson produced his key work on the meaning and mission of the Church, *The New Reformation?*[3] This is not to suggest that Robinson depends heavily on Bonhoeffer for his doctrine of the Church. By his own admission, Bishop Robinson did not really read Bonhoeffer until the early fifties and the *Letters and Papers* did not really sink in until the illness that incapacitated him for several months, during which time he wrote *Honest to God*. But it is interesting to see that the spirit of all of Robinson's writings is very much in the tradition embraced by Bonhoeffer, and that Robinson's emerging doctrine of the Church was forged in a theological atmosphere which was largely independent of direct influence from the martyred Lutheran theologian.

Just as *Honest to God* exemplifies the first major question concerning the secular meaning of the Gospel, *The New Reformation?* provides a splendid idea of the nature and dimensions of the second major problem: the secular mission of the Church. Although Robinson is theologically comfortable with the idea of the Church as the Body of Christ and 'the dedicated nucleus of those who actively acknowledge Jesus as Lord and have committed themselves to membership and mission within the visible sacramental fellowship of the Spirit' (p. 48), his main insistence is that the Church is a servant community which exists in and for the world, but ultimately for the sake of the Kingdom of God.[4]

This is not to suggest that the Church, as instrument of the Kingdom and servant of God in the world, is the only agent of God in history. It is the perennial temptation of the Church to believe this, 'to assume that what God is doing in this world he must be doing through the Church, that the space to watch, as it were, if one really wants to see what God is up to, is the Church papers.'[5] Nowhere in the Bible is it claimed that the Church is the mainspring of divine activity in history. The Church is but the world's deacon, a leavening influence in the body of history, serving within and not alongside the structures of the world.

And yet to larger and larger numbers of our generation, the Christian Gospel, in the manner and form in which it has been preached, is no longer the good news (which is part of the problem of the secular meaning of the Gospel), and the Church itself, to the extent that it is identified almost exclusively with the function of proclaiming the Word and duly administering the sacraments, has also become progressively more irrelevant. Today's religious question is not the question of the Reformers, 'How can I find a gracious God?' but 'How can I find a gracious neighbor?' *The* gracious neighbor, of course, is Jesus of Nazareth, 'the man for others'. He comes to us not as the Son of God, demanding acknowledgment of his Lordship, but as the Son of Man, as the stranger who comes alongside us in our questioning and in our sadness. 'It is only from there, as the man for others and with others, that he can make himself known to them as the Messiah of whom their Scriptures spoke.'[6] The primary task of the Church is to make such a meeting possible again. The Church must itself *be* the Son of Man on earth, an open society, an accepting community, whose chief characteristic is that it is prepared to meet men where they are and accept them for what they are.[7] For mankind will ultimately be judged by its own humanity, by what it really means to be a man, and 'it will understand that truth and accept it only as it *actually finds itself convicted by the Son of Man on earth*, that is, by the Church as she takes a towel and girds herself, by her ministers and her members as they "do judgment" for the least of his brethren'.[8]

But the Church has failed to project this image, and the tendency of the Reformation – Counter Reformation era was to think of the Church in terms of the gathered or the excommunicating group. 'It *defined* the Church when it was out of the world, as the salt piled, clean and white, in the cellar, as the leaven unmixed with the meal. And this is precisely when it is *not* being itself or performing its essential function. For it is distinctively itself when it cannot be seen and tasted for itself at all, but when it is transforming whatever it is in.'[9] The Church is not a circle of light surrounded on all sides by darkness, nor is Christ contained only within the circle of the Christian community. The Church is not a community gathered apart from and over against the non-churched world, and the last thing the Church exists to be is 'an organization for the religious',[10] whose main function is 'to make or keep men religious'.[11] On the contrary, 'its charter is to be the servant of the world'.[12]

The Church's primary task is not the expansion of her perimeter but the extension of God's Kingdom. For men are not judged ultimately by their distance from the visible Church, but by their distance from the Kingdom. In fact, from the beginning to end the Bible consistently visualizes the covenant people as a minority instrument of the Kingdom, whose minority status is not a scandal. Not all men are called to the Church; all men *are* called to the Kingdom. The Church, however, must make it possible for men to confront the power of the Gospel and thereby enter into the Kingdom of God. The Church accomplishes this by preaching the Gospel to the poor and, as often as necessary, in the nonreligious or secular terms which Jesus himself employed: the release of prisoners and the recovery of sight for the blind (cf. Lk 4:18), even if they never say, 'Lord, Lord.'

Consequently, if the Gospel is to become once again the good news of salvation, it must be proclaimed with a consciousness of the radically changed situation, in terms of an age of secularization. Christ must be allowed to confront men once again as the Son of Man through a Church which must be the servant of God in the world.

As the Church proceeds into this new era, it must be prepared for a radical stripping down and reformation of structures. Robinson has asked if the Church is *free* enough to be there in the midst of all the ambiguities of the 'secular hope', if the Church can allow itself to 'take shape around his servant presence in the world'. His faith is that the Church can do all of these things—'just'. 'And that is why,' he concludes, 'I believe in a new Reformation as a real and exciting divine possibility.'[13]

Cox

The discussion of the secular mission of the Church in American theology tends to be somewhat 'Low-Church' and reductionist. Harvey Cox represents the former tendency, and the 'death-of-God' theologians the latter.

Cox believes, and with good reason, that 'the theologians of our generation have tended to be inordinately obsessed with various aspects of the doctrine of the Church. ... [But] a doctrine of the Church is a secondary and derivative aspect of theology which comes *after* a discussion of God's action in calling man to cooperation in the bringing of the Kingdom. It comes after, not before, a clarification of the idea of the Kingdom and the appropriate response to the Kingdom in a particular era.'[14] In his initial premise, therefore, Cox's position is remarkably similar to Bishop Robinson's.

Cox is also very much in harmony with the general line of thought adopted at the Second Vatican Council when he insists that the Church is not, in the first instance, an institution but a people, the People of God. The Church is like a 'floating crap game' which moves 'where the action is'. Theology must be concerned first with discovering where the action is, and only then can it begin the work of shaping a Church which can get into the action. That is, 'a theology of social change must precede a theology of the Church' (p. 126). This is another way of saying that the question of the secular meaning of the Gospel must precede the question of the secular mission of the Church.

The content of the Church's ministry, for Dr Cox, is simply the continuation of Jesus' ministry, and that is aptly summarized in Lk 4:18, 19 (a text also cited by Robinson). Jesus thought of his task as threefold. He was to announce the arrival of the new régime. He was to personify its meaning. And he was to begin distributing its benefits. The Church shares this threefold responsibility, as 'the *avant-garde* of the new régime': *kerygma* (proclamation), *diakonia* (reconciliation, healing, and other forms of service), and *koinonia* (demonstration of the character of the new society).

With regard to its first task, the Church must tell the world what is going on and what to expect next. It broadcasts the fact that a revolution is under way and that the decisive battle has already taken place. 'In traditional language, the message of the Church is that God has defeated the "principalities and powers" by Jesus and has made it possible for man to become the "heir", the master of the created world. . . . These "principalities and powers" actually signify all the forces in a culture which cripple and corrupt human freedom' (p. 128). Through Jesus, man now has the power and the mission to rule over these forces and to use them in responsibility before God. In political terms, the revolutionary régime has seized power but the symbols of authority are still in the hands of the old displaced rulers. We are now in-between-the-times: between the achievement of *de facto* power and the appearance of visible *de jure* authority, between the resurrection and the second coming of the Lord.

It is not enough that the Church simply proclaim these facts to the world. She must also put her body where her preaching is. She must actually get down into the dirt and grime of history and participate in the great task of remaking the world into God's own Kingdom. This second responsibility of the Church is her mission of *diakonia*, of healing and reconciling, of unifying and binding up wounds. In a word, the Church must be the Good Samaritan in history, demonstrating by the quality and kind of her concerns and efforts the real meaning of her preaching.

And finally, the Church has the responsibility to provide a

visible demonstration of what she is saying in her *kerygma* and pointing to in her *diakonia*. The Church becomes the 'hope made visible', a kind of living picture of the character and composition of the true city of man for which the Church strives, what Karl Barth calls 'God's provisional demonstration of his intention for all humanity'.

The Church, then, must be one of the major signs of the Kingdom, but only *one* of the signs. The Church is not itself the Kingdom. Its whole existence is a derivative one, dependent entirely on the prior reality of the Kingdom. 'The *avant-garde* of God makes its announcement by allowing its own life to be shaped by the future Kingdom (not past tradition) and by indicating with its lips and its life where other signs of the Kingdom are appearing' (p. 147).

Cox makes no mention at all of the Church's sacramental dimension nor of her mysterious identification with Christ himself. He draws his ecclesiology in exclusively functional or operative terms. The Church *is* its mission. Unlike Bishop Robinson, Cox seems to accord little place to liturgy and hierarchical ministry. His interest in finding a biblical (Old Testament) foundation for his concept of secularization was not matched when he had to address himself to the problem of the Church. His references to the New Testament, while appropriate, are sketchy. He seems to confirm, inversely, Bishop Robinson's own dictum, that 'it is impossible to be a biblical theologian without being a High-Churchman'.[15]

Some of Cox's critics detected an anti-institutionalism in his ecclesiology and he responded to the charge in the Afterword to *The Secular City Debate*: 'I never intended to be anti-institutional, anarchistic or individualistic in *The Secular City*, but at times I allowed myself to use phrases which gave people that impression. I realize that the Church is not pure spirit and cannot live in the modern world, or in any world for that matter, without some institutional expression. . . . Institution is for man what instinct is for animal. Institutions make it possible for the organism to deal with certain levels of decisions by answering a whole range of questions before they are asked. . . . What we need now is a willingness to *reinstitutionalize* the forms of Church life based on a conscious theological recognition of what the Church's purpose is' (pp. 186–7). Which is to say, in the terms of my own book, that we must conduct the Einsteinian Revolution within the Church only in the light of, and with complete appreciation for, its prior Copernican Revolution. Our problem today, as I suggested in the Introduction, is that the Einsteinian Revolution is outstripping the Copernican. We are in a period of rapid change and theological immaturity. The combination is disastrous.

'Death-of-God' Theologians

Harvey Cox may sit lightly to the catholic elements of the Church (liturgy, sacraments, ordained ministry, and episcopacy for example), but his concept of the Church's mission is orthodox in the best sense of the word. He addresses himself to the traditional tasks of the Church (*kerygma, diakonia,* and *koinonia*), while reinterpreting them from within a secular context. Cox has offered only a partial ecclesiology, but, given the nature of the theological enterprise, that is all any theologian can hope for. The important thing is that the fragments be assimilable into the larger framework.

The 'death-of-God' theologians, on the other hand, do not seem interested in gathering up fragments for anything but a theological fire.[16] Thomas Altizer proposes that 'a truly contemporary theology can only begin its task today by first seeking a ground outside of the given and established form of the Church',[17] and he proceeds out of the assumption that 'the original Christian heresy was the identification of the Church with the body of Christ.'[18]

Altizer insists in his *Gospel of Christian Atheism* and in his earlier *Mircea Eliade and the Dialectic of the Sacred*[19] that the death of God is an historical event. 'We must acknowledge, therefore, that if God has died in our history, then insofar as the Church has entered history, it has become a corpse—as Kierkegaard knew so deeply. . . . In this situation, Christianity is increasingly becoming yet another Gnostic way of retreat from history.'[20] The radical Christian, therefore, must not be thought of as a reformer (for Altizer, unlike Robinson, there is no possibility or even desirability of a 'new Reformation'). The radical Christian is and must be a revolutionary, given to a total transformation of Christianity.[21] Christian radicalism, therefore, cannot coexist with the naïve and theologically erroneous view that the Church is the Body of Christ. Altizer believes that such an identification of Christ and the Church inevitably sets the Body of Christ apart from and even opposed to the body of humanity. 'Once the Church had claimed to be the body of Christ, it had already set upon the imperialistic path of conquering the world, of bringing the life and movement of the world into submission to the inhuman authority and power of an infinitely distant Creator and Judge.'[22]

With Altizer, we see how the various possibilities in Bonhoeffer's thought can even be employed against the stated purposes of Bonhoeffer's program, i.e., to make over the Church into the image of Jesus, 'the man for others'. The work of Bishop Robinson, and even of Harvey Cox, demonstrates that one can share the radically secular ethic of the 'death-of-God' theologian without thereby selling out on the first eighteen centuries of Christian tradition, while at the same time according some significant role to the

Church, whether as the Body of Christ and instrument of the Kingdom (Bishop Robinson) or as the *avant-garde* of the Kingdom (Harvey Cox). Reflection on the 'death-of-God' position, however, should serve as a sobering reminder that the investigation into the possibility of a secular meaning for the Gospel need not necessarily lead into a renewed theology of the Church. The question of the Church indeed flows from the question of the secular meaning of the Gospel, but we should be aware that it is possible to opt out of the issue entirely by doing what Altizer, and to a lesser extent Hamilton and van Buren, have done; namely, to discount the Church completely and bluntly characterize it as the corpse of God.

Catholic Theology Before Vatican II

For most Catholics (and for most Christians, Catholic or not) the question of the Church is no problem at all. We did not really need an ecumenical council to tell us what the Church is all about. The Church is an organization founded by Christ to provide us with the means of salvation. Her primary mission is to offer these means to as many people as possible. Her charter is, in a sense, to make and keep men 'religious'.

I am not about to suggest that the Church, and specifically Catholic theology, has suddenly become indifferent to the problem of salvation. But there are, in the position suggested above, certain underlying assumptions which demand some qualification. Some of these assumptions have already been challenged by certain Anglican and Protestant theologians, and these have been discussed throughout these chapters. What is significant in our time is that similar challenges, independently formulated, have been forthcoming from the Catholic side of the Reformation divide. Some of the freshest thinking on this question has come, not unexpectedly, from the Austrian Jesuit, Karl Rahner.

Every great religion, Rahner argues, has had its 'Middle Ages', i.e., its period of cultural, political, and social supremacy. Christianity has already passed through her own 'Middle Ages' and is now entering the age of *diaspora*, living within a pluralistic framework, numerically and culturally a minority.

This situation *ought not to be*, i.e., all nations and all mankind should accept the Gospel of Christ and become members of his Church; but, on the other hand, the *diaspora* situation is not something which *simply is*, something to be endured and protested against until some real improvement occurs. Rahner argues that there is a third possibility: the *diaspora* situation is a *must* in the history of salvation. It ought not to be, yet it must be so. And there are other examples of such *musts*: 'the poor you will always have with you'; the inevitability of scandals and schisms; and the supreme instance, the Cross itself. Jesus ought not to have been crucified, but it had to be so for the redemption of the world.

The old world order disintegrated with the Reformation, the Renaissance, the Enlightenment, and the French Revolution. The Church was no longer the Church of a closed culture. When the medieval culture became the vehicle for world-wide expansion, the Church moved with it into the world at large. 'In the moment when she begins to be a Church of *all* the heathen, she also begins, everywhere, to be a Church *among the heathen*.'[23]

The Christian faith in this new situation lacks the usual institutional and sociological support. It must become a matter of personal choice and free decision. The Church will bear the marks of a sect rather than of a Church 'in possession'. The Church of the *diaspora* will be more immediately religious.

Rahner argues that we must adjust to this new situation without compromising our missionary fervor. It is a question of priorities and values. What we seek is not quantity (for where is it said that we must have the whole 100 per cent), but quality, authentic Christians who will live the Gospel and give effective witness to Christ. 'Even in the *diaspora* the initiative can really be ours.'

Rahner's position closely parallels the views of Bonhoeffer, Cox, and Robinson. Bonhoeffer had argued that the world has 'come of age' and he drew his conclusions accordingly; Rahner notes that the Church has come out of her 'Middle Ages' and into a *diaspora* situation. Cox describes the development of the secular city in terms similar in many respects to Rahner's description of the *diaspora*, of the Church's emergence from her 'Middle Ages'. And both theologians seem to view this phenomenon as a *must* in the history of salvation. Bishop Robinson lays great stress on the fact that the Church is the instrument of the Kingdom of God, that the Church does not exist in and for herself. Rahner, too, proposes that the Church exists, not for her own sake, but to bring men to the love of God in Christ, which is the realization of the Kingdom. Citing St Augustine, Rahner reminds us: 'Many whom God has, the Church does not have; and many whom the Church has, God does not have.'[24]

Some biblical support for Rahner's position is offered, independently, by Yves Congar, O.P., in the first three chapters of his *Wide World, My Parish*. Congar insists that the fundamental biblical category is not quantity but 'the idea of representative elements having a universal dynamic value'. Consequently, the Church must be viewed as a minority community in the service of the majority. 'The Church exists in herself, but she does not exist *for* herself;

she has a mission to and a responsibility for the world. . . .'[25]

Other Catholic theologians have emphasized the sacramental dimension of the Church and have described its mission essentially in these terms. Thus, Edward Schillebeeckx, O.P., suggests that the Church must offer itself as the sacrament of encounter with God in Christ, 'a visible invitation to men to accept charity'.[26] A similar approach, from the vantage point of a theology of revelation rather than ecclesiology as such, is fashioned by René Latourelle, S.J., who implies that the Church's fundamental mission is the erection of signs of authentic Christian holiness in the world.[27]

Second Vatican Council

Whereas the 'conventional wisdom' growing out of a particular kind of theology has always insisted that the Church's primary, if not exclusive, mission is to increase and multiply through conversion and baptism, contemporary Catholic theology (Rahner, Congar, and others) seems willing to accord her a larger task. This is to serve and to bear witness. The Church is to be both a servant and a sign. How these changing concepts of the Church's mission are contained, explicitly or implicitly, in the documents of the Second Vatican Council will be the concern of Part III of this book. However, for the sake of providing a fuller and clearer picture of the actual state of the discussion in Catholic thought, a summary of the council's doctrine is offered here.

The council recognized that the situation in the world has changed and that it is no longer possible to ignore the fundamental responsibilities of the Church in areas which transcend the purely 'religious' (such as liturgy and sacramental ministration). 'The Church has always had the duty of scrutinizing the signs of the times and of interpreting them in the light of the Gospel' (*The Church in the Modern World*, art. 4). For the council, the 'signs of the times' are these: the transition of the human race from 'a rather static concept of reality to a more dynamic, evolutionary one'; changes in the traditional local communities; the growth of industrialization; the increase of urbanization; new and more efficient media of social, economic, and technological progress; the phenomenon of 'socialization'; a movement toward 'more mature and personal exercise of liberty' (see arts. 5 and 6; see also arts. 7, 34, 39, and 40). In response to this new situation the Second Vatican Council insists that the Church must live as God's Suffering Servant: 'Inspired by no other earthly ambition, the Church seeks but a solitary goal: to carry forward the work of Christ under the lead of the befriending Spirit. And Christ entered this world to give witness to the truth, to rescue and not to sit in judgment, to serve and not to be served' (art. 3; see also art. 40 and 45).

The service orientation is also clearly evident in the discussion of authority in the central decree on the Church, *Lumen Gentium*. The faithful in general, the bishops, his priests and deacons, and all ministers of the Church must exercise their responsibilities as servants, one of another (e.g., 'all the faithful of Christ of whatever rank or status . . . must devote themselves with all their being to the glory of God and the service of their neighbor'—art. 40; see also arts. 27, 28, 29, and 41).

If the Church does indeed live as a Servant Church, it will be the most effective sign of the Gospel of Christ and the coming of the Kingdom of God. 'For it is the function of the Church . . . to make God the Father and his Incarnate Son present and in a sense visible. This result is achieved chiefly by the witness of a living and mature faith. . . . This faith needs to prove its fruitfulness by penetrating the believer's entire life, including its worldly dimensions, and by activating him toward justice and love, especially regarding the needy' (*Church in Modern World*, art. 21; see also art. 93).

Catholic Theology After Vatican II

There is some evidence that Catholic theology is beginning to move beyond Vatican II, which remains largely in the Reformation, neo-orthodox, Barthian tradition: kerygmatic, Christocentric, and biblical. A major contribution is being made by J. B. Metz, discussed in Chapter 1. Metz's concept of the Church is closely patterned after Moltmann's. For both, the Church is primarily an exodus community, the pilgrim People of God, which exists to proclaim the hope of all mankind in the coming of the Kingdom of God. The Church's distinctive responsibility today is social criticism and prophetic utterance. Its goal is always the future realization of the Kingdom of God.

Metz seems to be alone in the field of Catholic theology in recognizing the fundamental relationship between the Church and the Kingdom of God, and in criticizing the inadequacies of the council's ecclesiology. Robert Adolfs has made some effort to emphasize the servant character of the Church and he succeeds in focusing the issue more sharply than did the council. However, his book, *The Grave of God*, is essentially a popular work and it fails to deal systematically with the eschatological dimension.

One final indication of the present course of Catholic ecclesiology is to be found in a place which ordinarily would escape the attention of most Christians, indeed of most Catholics. At the beginning of Advent in 1966, Richard Cardinal Cushing, the archbishop of Boston, issued a pastoral letter entitled *The Servant Church* in which all the major themes of contemporary ecclesiology are developed and employed. The document suggests at the outset that it is impossible to understand the mission of the Church apart from the mission of Jesus himself, and that it is furthermore impossible to understand *his* mission without reference to the Kingdom of God. The Church, therefore, must be a servant Church, fulfilling the mission of the Suffering Servant of God, whose Body it is. The mission and ministry of the Church make sense only in terms of its threefold relationship to the Kingdom of God: to proclaim the Kingdom, to work and struggle to bring it about here and now, and finally to be a sign of the Kingdom in our own time. In developing this position, the pastoral letter draws upon the insights of Bonhoeffer, Cox, Robinson, and, to varying degrees, the other theologians mentioned above, even to the extent of endorsing—with some qualification—Bonhoeffer's idea of 'religionless Christianity'.

While the pastoral letter does go beyond the ecclesiology of Vatican II and makes much more explicit the servant character of the Church as well as its fundamental and normative relationship to the Kingdom of God, the document stops short of calling for a Copernican Revolution (and its logically subsequent Einsteinian Revolution). This is understandable in view of the specific aim of the letter, which was pastoral rather than doctrinal. Its principal concern was to shed some light on the pressing social, economic, and political issues of the day.

A genuinely radical theology of the Church, however, must have an eschatological context. It must insist upon the relativity of the Church's place in history and upon its essential subordination to the Kingdom of God. Not all men are called to the Church, nor is the Church the ordinary means of salvation. The full assimilation of these premises within the Christian community will require nothing less than a theological Copernican Revolution. Stubborn resistance, on the other hand, will succeed only in leaving the Church at least four centuries behind, reducing it eventually to impotence in the face of its multiple contemporary tasks. The likelihood of such resistance should not be discounted in a cavalier or falsely optimistic fashion. The lesson of Galileo remains a judgment upon the Church for all time. And Galileo, after all, was condemned for daring to teach the Copernican theory. The effort to dislodge the Church from the center of history will undoubtedly create as many cries of anguish and condemnation as Galileo's earlier suggestion that the earth is not at the center of the universe.

Nor should we forget that we shall not have achieved too much, once we have reconciled ourselves to this Copernican Revolution. This will bring us abreast of the sixteenth century, at just about the point when Copernicus proposed his theory and Protestantism raised its head in judgment upon the Church. The Einsteinian Revolution remains our unfinished business, as we enter a time of rapid change and of structural upheaval.

Part Two

BIBLICAL
AND POSTBIBLICAL
THEOLOGIES OF THE CHURCH

Chapter 3

The Church of the New Testament

I should be clear, at the outset, about the aims and point of Part II. It is not meant to be a superficial history of ecclesiology, a clever reworking of the summaries of biblical theologians and historians of Christian theology, nor is it constructed simply to offer some historical background for the general argument of the book. I hope to establish, at least partially and perhaps only tentatively, that the pre-Copernican notion of the Church is not demanded by the classical ecclesiologies, and especially the normative ecclesiology of the New Testament. This is a modest and minimal goal, and it will be achieved, if at all, indirectly. More positively, I shall argue that every distortion or exaggeration concerning the nature and mission of the Church, from both Catholic and Protestant sides, springs from a failure to safeguard and preserve the delicate balance between two key biblical notions: the Body of Christ and the Kingdom of God.

The image of the Body of Christ emphasizes the identification of Christ and the Church and refers to the Church as a communion, a community-at-rest, so to speak. Serious theological reflection on the concept of the Body of Christ should exercise a countervailing force against a tendency, common among some Protestant theologians, to view the Church in exclusively functional or missionary terms.[1] The idea of the Kingdom of God, which was central to the teaching of Jesus, serves, on the other hand, to illuminate the dichotomy and the distinction between Christ and the Church. Furthermore, the Church-Kingdom relationship emphasizes, as the body-image does not (at least on the surface), that the Church is, indeed, essentially missionary and that her mission is not inner-directed but outer-directed, i.e., Kingdom-directed. Such reflection, of course, proves to be an effective antidote to the common Catholic tendency toward triumphalism and juridicism in its concept of the Church. Once this fundamental link between Church and Kingdom is seen in its proper proportion, the Copernican and the Einsteinian Revolutions are theologically inevitable.

I shall also attempt in this Part to portray the kind of pre-Copernican ecclesiology that developed as a result of the canonical and polemical concerns of the Counter Reformation period. I refer to this ecclesiological deviation as Ptolemaic ecclesiology and to its creature as the Ptolemaic Church. I shall be arguing, in Part III, that the Second Vatican Council's theology of the Church is lodged somewhere between the Ptolemaic and the Copernican Revolutions. The final Part IV, and indeed the very argument of the book itself, attempts the task of dislodgement.

As Dietrich Bonhoeffer's earlier Christological writings become more widely read and more thoroughly understood, he may become something of an embarrassment to those who now celebrate—on the sole basis of his *Letters and Papers from Prison*—his radical vision of God, the Gospel, and the Church.[2] Bonhoeffer is not an uncritical functionalist in his theology. He has argued, for example, that while the person and work of Christ (Christology and soteriology) cannot ultimately be separated, the Christological question nonetheless has theological priority over the soteriological question. 'If I know *who* the person is who does this I will also know *what* he does.'[3]

Bonhoeffer's basic theological conservatism comes through as well in his discussion of the Church as the sacrament of Christ:

> Christ the sacrament is also there in and as the community. The sacrament already in itself has a physical form which goes beyond the Word. The community is the body of Christ. Body here is not just a metaphor. The community *is* the body of Christ, it does not *represent* the body of Christ. Applied to the community, the concept of the body is not just a functional concept which merely refers to the members of this body; it is a comprehensive and central concept of the mode of existence of the one who is present in his exaltation and his humiliation. . . . Christ is not only the head of the community but also the community itself. (Cf. 1 Cor. 12 and the Epistle to the Ephesians.) Christ is head and every member.[4]

Indeed, Bonhoeffer can even be cited on the side of pre-Copernican ecclesiology (although the main thrust of all his work provides a more proper context for the statement): 'Since Christ is present in the Church after the cross and the resurrection, this Church too must be understood as the centre of history.'[5]

The point of these introductory remarks is to suggest that even such a thoroughgoing, functional ecclesiology as that fashioned by Bonhoeffer and his disciples cannot completely and absolutely eschew the Catholic elements of the Church. To paraphrase Bonhoeffer's views on the Christology-soteriology relationship, it is impossible to raise the issue of what the Church does without also asking what the Church is. This is the perennial Protestant temptation, and even Catholic secularizers and functionalists could easily yield to it. Accordingly, serious theological reflection on the

Body of Christ, as the community of grace, as the sacrament of salvation, and so forth, is no idle, intramural activity. The theologian neglects this essential aspect of the Church at the peril of distorting the whole reality and of reducing ecclesiology to a series of moral exhortations for Church mission. But this is not to endorse the excessive and one-sided Mystical Body theology of several Catholic theologians. This should become apparent in Chapter 4, where I shall offer a critique of the ecclesiology of Sebastian Tromp, S.J. Father Tromp provides an exceptionally apt test case because he is, in the first instance, a faithful disciple of Robert Bellarmine (who represents so well the polemical, canonical ecclesiology of the Counter Reformation), and, in the second instance, the chief architect of Pope Pius XII's encyclical letter on the Mystical Body, *Mystici Corporis* (1943).

The Church as the Body of Christ

Obviously, no attempt is being fashioned herein to propose a complete theology of the Body of Christ, or, indeed, a complete biblical ecclesiology. After all, 'the Church is everywhere present in the New Testament even where it is not manifest in concepts and imagery. The Church gave birth to the New Testament writings and they all bear witness to its existence and life.'[6] Admittedly, there are not very many complete biblical theologies of the Church, and fewer systematic ecclesiologies.[7] But our purposes here will be served adequately if we can summarize the current state of the discussion among New Testament scholars. I do this with the conviction that 'the innermost center of the Church's life would be overlooked if its relation to Christ were passed over in silence'.[8]

The prevailing Protestant exegesis in the period just

before the appearance of *Mystici Corporis* (1943) linked the Pauline concept of the Body of Christ with Gnostic mythology, and, more specifically, with the myth of the Heavenly Man (*Urmensch*) who comes to deliver the members of his body imprisoned in matter, to reintegrate them into his body of which he is the head.[9] Not unexpectedly, Rudolf Bultmann has made this connection with relentless consistency. For the Gnostic view it is essential that men be united in a substantial way with the Redeemer, so intimately, in fact, that together they constitute one body (*soma*). And just as the Redeemer is a cosmic figure, so, too, is his body. What happens to the Redeemer happens as well to the whole body. Thus, if he suffered death, the same is true of the body. If he was raised from the dead, the same is true for the body. 'And just as his return to the heavenly home as the "redeemed Redeemer" means his release from the sinister powers that rule the world below, likewise they who are bound up with him into one body share in this release or "redemption".'[10]

Over against both this Bultmannian view and the so-called 'traditional' Catholic opinion, that 'Body of Christ' refers only to a collectivity, have stood Lucien Cerfaux, Pierre Benoit, O.P., and John A. T. Robinson. A key text in Cerfaux's argument is 1 Cor 12:12–13a: 'For Christ is like a single body with its many limbs and organs, which, many as they are, together make up one body. For indeed we were all brought into one body by baptism.' Cerfaux proposes here that Paul is not speaking of anything so weak as a social organization or a collectivity, but that he has in mind the real, *physical* body of Christ. The Church is identified with Christ in a mystical way: 'As the glorified body of Christ is the full flowering of his person, so also is the Church. In the mystical order nothing is opposed to a true identification of the Church with the glorious body of Christ.'[11]

Although the terminology may be deceptively similar, Cerfaux's interpretation goes far deeper than the biblical exegesis which underlies the encyclical letter of Pope Pius XII.

Pierre Benoit also rejects the view that the 'Body of Christ' merely designates the organized society which is the Church. He, too, argues for a 'realistic' interpretation and he criticizes the adjective 'mystical' because it does not sufficiently portray the realism of the Pauline theology. In examining the body-image in 1 Cor 12:12–30, Benoit is in basic accord with Cerfaux's interpretation. Furthermore, he sees the body-image as central in both Colossians and Ephesians. Christ is the savior of the body (Eph 5:23); the body is his and we are his members (v. 30). It is this unique body into which we have been called (Col 3:15) and in which both Jews and Gentiles have been reconciled (Eph 2:16). It is a living organism, coherent and hierarchical, which gathers all Christians into it and which grows according to God's design (Col 2:19; Eph 4:16). In a word, it is the Church (Col 1:18; Eph 1:23; 5:23 ff.). Finally, it is a portion of the fullness (*pleroma*) of Christ (Col 1:18; 2:9; Eph 1:23; 4:13 ff.). It is not only a moral or a social body according to the classical metaphor of Gnostic mythology, but rather it is the personal body of Christ (Eph 2:16; Col 2:15–18), which effects a real, ontological union with Christ as head.[12]

The most complete study of the Pauline concept of the Body of Christ has been produced by John A. T. Robinson, the Bishop of Woolwich. 'The Christian,' he writes, 'because he is in the Church and united with him in the sacraments, is part of Christ's body so literally that all that happened in and through that body in the flesh can be repeated in and through him now'.[13] The body-concept is the linchpin of all Pauline thought and provides the point of departure for his ecclesiology. Moreover, Paul's orientation is consistently 'realistic'. He 'never speaks of "a body of Christians" but always of "the Body of Christ". For him, at any rate, the word clearly referred to the organism of a particular person.'[14]

In 1 Cor 6:15 St Paul asks: 'Do you not know that your bodies are limbs and organs of Christ?' The language here is violent and Robinson is convinced that Paul intended it to be violent. In Paul's mind, the Church is not something corporate but something corporeal:

> To say that the Church is the body of Christ is no more of a metaphor than to say that the flesh of the incarnate Jesus or the bread of the Eucharist is the body of Christ. None of them is 'like' his body (Paul never says this): each of them is the body of Christ, in that each is the physical complement of the one and the same Person and Life. . . . He is not saying anything so weak as that the Church is a society with a common life and governor, but that its unity is that of a single physical entity: disunion is dismemberment. For it is in fact no other than the glorified body of the risen and ascended Christ.[15]

Pauline realism is further demonstrated in his use of sexual imagery to describe the union of Christ and Church (Rom 7:4 ff.; 2 Cor 11:2; Eph 5:22-23). And it is in the light of this theological perspective that Paul's strictures against certain individualistic practices in connection with the Eucharist should be viewed (see 1 Cor 11:17-34). The offenders have no sense of the body and therefore are not worthy to eat the Lord's Supper and participate sacramentally in the Body of Christ.

While this expedition into the Pauline concept of the

Body of Christ has been brief and sketchy, it should be adequate for our modest purposes in Part II and in the book as a whole. What must be clear is that the contemporary functionalist theologian cannot simply ignore the data of the New Testament. He may wish to develop his own exegetical viewpoint, e.g., with Bultmann over against Robinson, but the functionalist must at least come to terms with the issue. For if, indeed, the Church is the Body of Christ in a sense which approximates the realistic interpretation of Cerfaux, Benoit, and Robinson, then it is theologically indefensible to construct an understanding of the Church which reduces it to a group of like-minded people who share a common mission or a common historical perspective (*blik*). As Bonhoeffer himself has argued in *Christ the Center*, the question of mission presupposes the question of essential nature. This community is so intimately identified with Jesus Christ that it can be called, and in fact has been called in the New Testament, the very Body of Christ. He is present in this community in a way which knows no duplication elsewhere.

It is on the basis of this particular biblical exegesis that a systematic theologian such as Karl Rahner is able to write:

This abiding presence of Christ in the Church is the sign that God in his merciful love identifies himself in Christ with the world. And because the Church is the sign of the grace of God definitively triumphant in the world in Christ, this sign can never—as a real possibility— become a meaningless symbol. . . . The Church is the official presence of the grace of Christ in the public history of the one human race. In its socially organized form the people of God, as in fact redeemed by Christ, receives his permanent presence through history.[16]

The Church and the Kingdom of God

The problem of the Kingdom of God has always been an issue of major importance and discussion in Christian biblical scholarship, especially among Protestants. There were some, earlier in the century, who insisted that, in the preaching of Jesus, the Kingdom of God is a purely *future* reality, that Jesus did not proclaim the reign of God as immediate and in no sense did he proclaim it as actually realized. The opposite point of view, maintained by C. H. Dodd, suggests that the Kingdom is *already realized* in Jesus and his ministry (particularly, his death and resurrection). The future will add nothing essentially new.[17] Other positions were developed between these two poles of thought.[18] Earlier Catholic scholarship rejected not only both extremes but also most of the options in between. Catholics insisted that the Kingdom of God is now permanently present in the Church and that it continues to develop both interiorly and exteriorly in the history of the Church. But current biblical studies emphasize the distinction between the Church and the Kingdom and they base their judgment, in part, on the fact that the final judgment will bring into the redeemed community of the perfect Kingdom other men who did not know Jesus in their lifetime and who evidently were not members of his visible community; and, on the other hand, unfaithful and unworthy members will be cast out (see Mt 25:34-40; also Mt 7:22 ff.; 13:24-30, 36-43, 47-50; 22:11-13; Lk 13:26 ff.).

But assuming that the Church and the Kingdom of God are not simply identical, then what *is* the precise relationship between the two realities? Contemporary biblical scholarship offers several possible answers.

For Rudolf Bultmann, whose perspective is existentialist,

time is not linear. The past, the present, and the future do not refer to successive stages on a continuous time-line, but rather are certain dimensions of a person's life. Thus, the past refers to the situation in which we find ourselves. It is an unfavorable situation and yet one for which we are not personally responsible. The present consists in the consciousness of our inability to escape from our predicament. And the future holds the possibilities of becoming something else, of doing something about the situation at hand. 'History is swallowed up by eschatology.'[19] There was never any question of Jesus' intending to establish a Church, for he shared the eschatological expectations of his contemporaries. He envisioned the inauguration of the Kingdom as 'a tremendous cosmic drama' which would occur in the immediate future. Shorn of its mythological world-view, the eschatological preaching of Jesus proclaimed 'the majesty of God and the inescapability of his judgment, and over against these the emptiness of the world and of men were felt with such an intensity that it seemed that the world was at an end, and that the hour of crisis was present'.[20]

Jesus is an eschatologist because he proclaims the will of God and the responsibility of man. Jesus Christ himself, in his person, his coming, his passion, and his glorification, is the eschatological event. And the eschatological event which is Jesus Christ 'happens here and now as the Word is being preached'.[21] The Word of God and the Church belong together, because the former constitutes the latter as the community of the elect. 'As the word is God's word only as an event, the Church is genuine Church only as an event which happens each time here and now; for the Church is the eschatological community of the saints, and it is only in a paradoxical way identical with the ecclesiastical institutions which we observe as social phenomena of secular history.'[22]

When viewed within the perspective of 'realized eschatology', the Church perpetually reconstitutes the crisis in which the Kingdom of God came in history. The Church does this especially at the Eucharist, but also through her preaching which is directed towards 'reconstituting in the experience of individuals the hour of decision which Jesus brought. Its underlying theme is always: "The time is fulfilled and the Kingdom of God has come; repent and believe the Gospel".'[23]

Dodd's thought is further developed by N. A. Dahl. To say that the Church is the 'eschatological community' means that the Church 'exists in the interval between Christ's death, resurrection and heavenly enthronement and his final revelation as Lord, Judge and Saviour; and not only his *parousia* but also his birth, death and resurrection are seen as messianic, "eschatological" events, happening "when the fullness of time was come", "in these last days".'[24] The Church in this perspective is something entirely new, a new creation (2 Cor 5:17).

Cullmann distinguishes not only between the Church and the Kingdom of God but also between the Kingdom of God and the Kingdom of Christ.[25] He suggests that while the Kingdom of Christ and the Church are distinct, they coincide chronologically. The Kingdom of God, on the other hand, is a purely future quantity. Because the Kingdom of Christ has already been inaugurated through the death and resurrection of Jesus, the Christian has reason to hope in the coming of the Kingdom of God. Christ's Kingdom will yield to God's Kingdom after the Second Coming.

The New Testament problem regarding the Kingdom of Christ is a problem of time, of the tension between present and future. If we do not develop a proper understanding of the Kingdom of Christ, then neither can we hope to bring forth an adequate concept of the Church, for 'the time of the Church can be defined in just the same way'.[26] It is the

Spirit which brings the future into the present, and it is the Spirit which is already present in the Church as a pledge of what is to come (2 Cor 2:22) and the first fruits of the future harvest (Rom 8:23).

Despite the similarities between the Church and the Kingdom of Christ, the Church is not to be regarded as a mere section of the Kingdom. The Church, according to Cullmann, represents the 'heart and center of the *Regnum Christi*'.[27] The Church 'forms the narrowly confined early setting of the *Regnum Christi* which Christ, the head of the whole creation, has chosen for his earthly body'.[28]

The Church must be seen in the context of the history of salvation. The Church, like Israel, is the remnant community, standing for all mankind. She is 'the earthly center from which the full Lordship of Christ becomes visible',[29] and this, in fact, is the essential mark of the Church: that she acknowledges the Lordship of Christ. The Church's task is the preaching of the Gospel to all and she must do this with the realization that the coming of the Kingdom of God will not depend on whether the Church is great or small on the day which God has appointed for the end of history.

Wolfhart Pannenberg has criticized all three major positions. Dodd and Bultmann exaggerate the difference between present and future in the preaching of Jesus concerning the Kingdom, to the degree of dismissing the futurity of the Kingdom of God as a remnant of Jewish thought. 'In abstracting the present impact from the whole of Jesus' message of the Kingdom, the message was grievously distorted,' Pannenberg has written. 'Jesus indeed spoke of the presence of the Kingdom of God, but always in terms of the presence of God's *coming* Kingdom. Futurity is fundamental for Jesus' message.' Pannenberg also disagrees with Cullmann's view that Jesus understood the Kingdom of God as beginning in his presence and only to be fulfilled in the future. 'It is more appropriate,' he suggests, 'to reverse the connection between present and future, giving priority to the future.' For Jesus, 'God's Kingdom does not lie in the distant future but is imminent. Thus, the present is not independent from that future. Rather does the future have an imperative claim upon the present, alerting all men to the urgency and exclusiveness of seeking first the Kingdom of God. As this message is proclaimed and accepted, God's rule is present and we can even now have a glimpse of his future glory. In this way we can see the present as an effect of the future, in contrast to the conventional assumption that past and present are the cause of the future.'[30] Therefore Pannenberg insists that the nature and mission of the Church cannot be understood except in relation to the future realization of the Kingdom, and every aspect of Church life and order has to be reevaluated in terms of this fundamental principle.[31]

Catholic theology no longer insists on the complete identification of Church and Kingdom. Few theologians (if any) would agree with F. M. Braun's judgment that the Protestant refusal to identify Church and Kingdom violates the incarnational principle of the Gospel and of revelation.[32] Nor would they readily accept the view of Charles Journet which attributes the Protestant position to their doctrine of imputed justice and to their fear that an identification of Church and Kingdom might lead to the confusion of the Kingdom of God with that of this world and of the political order.

More moderate Catholic positions have been advanced by Lucien Cerfaux and A. Feuillet. Cerfaux, like Cullmann, introduces the distinction between the Kingdom of Christ and the Kingdom of God. The Church is the Kingdom of Christ because of the sanctifying power of Christ that exists within it, and yet the Kingdom of Christ and the Kingdom of God are not identical. Feuillet, too, qualifies his suggestion that the Church and the Kingdom are one and the same reality. The Church is both the actualization on earth of the Kingdom of God and yet is always at its service. The Church is not an end in itself but has, instead, a supra-terrestrial finality, for she is oriented toward the consummation of the Kingdom of God.

Rudolf Schnackenburg represents the best Catholic position on this question. 'God's reign,' he writes, 'is not so associated with the Church that we can speak of it as a "present form of God's Kingdom", since this would suppose an amalgamation with the Church's history on earth. God's reign as such has no organization and goes through no process; it does not embrace the just and sinners, it is in no sense dependent upon earthly and human factors. It is not "built up" by men and thus brought to its goal. Yet all this can be said of the Church in its mundane form. . . .'[33]

Furthermore, as I suggested earlier, the Last Judgment will bring into the redeemed community of the perfect Kingdom other men who did not join the Church in their lifetime (Mt 25:34-40), while, on the other hand, some Church members will be rejected and cast out (Mt 7:22 ff., etc.). Consequently, membership in the Church does not guarantee affiliation with either the present or the future Kingdom, nor does life apart from the Church indicate exclusion from the Kingdom.

The Church is the instrument of the Kingdom of God, for Christ has chosen her as his direct sphere of operation in ruling the cosmos. 'Christ's reign over the world is realized in a special manner in the Church and becomes there a concrete reality of grace. . . . Through the Church Christ wins increasingly his dominion over all things and draws them ever more powerfully and completely beneath himself as head.'[34] The Church and the cosmos are not identical; however, the Church does assume 'cosmic significance', for it is in and through the Church that the cosmos is grasped by Christ. The Church, therefore, has by her very existence and in her very nature an essential relation to the world and hence a special task and mission.

For Bishop Robinson, the Church is the society in which the universal reign of God in Christ is acknowledged and in which this reign, is, or should be, embodied more fully than in any other section of humanity. It is the instrument by which the rest of creation is to be restored and conformed to the image of the Son, but in fulfilling this instrumental role the Church must resist the 'perennial temptation . . . to equate itself with the Kingdom of God on earth, and so to regard itself as the only agent of God in this world'.[35] Just as the ministry is a function of, and therefore subordinate to, the Church, so the Church is a function of, and subordinate to, the Kingdom of God. 'The Kingdom of God, rather even than the People of God, is the controlling category of biblical theology for both Old and New Testaments.'[36] The reign of God has been realized once and for all in history by means of Christ's victory, and it is the task of the Church to translate this victory into open acknowledgment and moral obedience. This means that the Church stands always under the judgment of the Kingdom.

Indeed, the very key to understanding Robinson's entire theology of the Church is the formula: 'Have as high a doctrine of the Ministry as you like, as long as your doctrine of the Church is higher; and have as high a doctrine of the Church as you like, as long as your doctrine of the Kingdom is higher.' And yet, as Robinson has observed, 'the doctrine of the Church has never consistently been worked out from the end of the Kingdom: the Kingdom has regularly been seen from the end of the Church'.[37]

An apt synthesis of the New Testament concept of the Kingdom of God and its special relationship to the Church is contained in the fifth article of the Second Vatican Council's *Dogmatic Constitution on the Church* (to which I shall be referring in greater detail in Part III). The Constitution reminds us that the very heart of Jesus' preaching was the coming of the Kingdom of God: 'The time is fulfilled, and the Kingdom of God is at hand' (Mk 1:15; Mt 4:17). The Kingdom was clearly present in the *word* of Christ, in his proclamation of the gospel of salvation. 'Those who hear the word with faith and become part of the little flock of Christ (Lk 12:32), have received the Kingdom itself.'

The Kingdom is also manifested in the *work* of the Lord. 'If I cast out devils by the finger of God, then the Kingdom of God has come upon you' (Lk 11:20; Mt 12:28). And when the disciples of John the Baptist asked Jesus if he was the one who was to come, or were they to look for another, he answered not in abstract language but in secular terms: 'Go back and report to John what you hear and see: the blind recovering their sight, cripples walking, lepers being cleansed, the deaf hearing, dead men being raised to life, the poor hearing the good news' (Mt 11:5; Lk 4:18–19). These are among the most important passages in the entire New Testament. If the heart of Jesus' preaching and ministry was the Kingdom of God, then it is important that we be able to detect the signs of the Kingdom as it comes into existence. And the business of the Church is to erect these signs.

Finally, the presence of the Kingdom is clearly visible in the very *person* of Christ, who came 'not to be served, but to serve and to give his life as a ransom for many' (Mk 19:45). 'His life, in a very real sense, is the first fruits of the perfect realization of the Kingdom that we will know at the end of time. He directs us how to seek after the Kingdom and shows what it means to be a truly human being, a "man for others". This is the fabric of which the Kingdom is made;

life in Christ is life after the pattern of God's own Kingdom.'[38]

What is to be the specific relationship, then, between the Kingdom which Christ preaches, inaugurates, and personifies, and the Church, which is his very Body? This same fifth article of the council's document on the Church notes that the Church 'receives the mission to proclaim and to establish among all peoples the Kingdom of Christ and of God and makes up the germ and beginning of that Kingdom on earth'. Insofar as the Christian community embodies the love of Christ and is an image of the Gospel itself, the Kingdom of God is present to it. But the Church and the Kingdom of God are not simply coextensive. The Kingdom is larger and greater than the Church. Indeed, the Church is subordinate to the Kingdom.

'While it slowly grows,' the council document continues, 'the Church strains toward the completed Kingdom and, with all its strength, hopes and desires to be united in glory with its King.' The Church, in other words, lives in a state of tension: between the 'already' and the 'not yet', between 'promise' and 'fulfillment', between the 'Kingdom-realized' and the 'Kingdom-to-be-realized'. The Church lives with a spirit of joy, because her faith is grounded on the Risen Christ (see Rom 4:25); but she also lives with a spirit of hope, because much lies yet in the future; Christ will not be 'all in all' until the end of history.[39]

The Church, therefore, carries on her work with a sense of theological realism. She is, indeed, the Body of Christ and that small segment of mankind which alone publicly acknowledges that Jesus is the Lord. She must preach this; she must spend herself as a suffering servant that others may see the real meaning of the Gospel; and she must live in such a way that her life as a community would not make sense if Jesus is not the Risen Lord.

But the Church must also have a sense of humility about her mission. She is, in fact, the Body of Christ, but she is not thereby an end in herself. She exists for the sake of the Kingdom, and she works with the realization that many will come to the Kingdom apart from her, that 'many whom God has, the Church does not have' (St Augustine). It should be clear that the central questions of Church membership and mission cannot be understood properly apart from the fundamental relationship between the Church and the Kingdom of God.

In summary: no convincing case can be made from the New Testament that all men are called to membership in the Church. All men are, indeed, called to accept and live the Gospel and thereby to create and enter into God's Kingdom, but the Church and the Kingdom are not one and the same reality. At the Last Judgment there will be the separating of the sheep from the goats. Membership in the Church is no guarantee of affiliation with the Kingdom, either now or hereafter. What comes through from the pages of Sacred Scripture, both Old and New Testament, is not that God wants all men to become Israel or the new Israel, but that God wants all men to acknowledge his dominion over them. Israel and the Church are but his instruments. God reigns when his will is accepted and lived, if only implicitly. And his will is that we should love one another, as he loves us in Christ. Consequently, when men take a genuine interest in and concern for the needs of one another, God's will is being realized and his Kingdom comes into being (see Gal. 6:2). The Church's task is to be the public sign and instrument of the Kingdom.

But it is pointless to accord such a function to the Church if it is nothing more or less than a humanitarian social agency, or a group of like-minded individuals sharing a common perspective and moving here and there, wherever 'the action is'. If the theological reality of the Church goes no deeper than that, there seems little reason to perpetuate this community in history or to continue one's personal affiliation with it. It is because the Christian believes that the Church is the Body of Christ that he attributes any ultimate significance to its mission in the world.

However, when the Church of the New Testament is pushed beyond the borders of theological interest and discussion, the beginning of the end is at hand. This has already happened in the work of Thomas Altizer, and it was inevitable. He dismissed the first eighteen centuries of Christian tradition and rejected any normative character for Sacred Scripture. Not only does he wipe out any trace of the Body of Christ, but even the dynamic relationship between Church and Kingdom is dissolved. Altizer had nothing else to do but declare the Church to be the corpse of the dead God. This is an extreme development, of course, but every functionalist must be aware of this proclivity within his own secular ecclesiology.

On the other hand, the failure to relate the Church as the Body of Christ to the Kingdom of God, and further, to respect the dichotomy between Church and Kingdom, has produced its own kind of extreme distortion. If the Church is the Body of Christ alone, it is subordinate to nothing and responsible to nothing. All men must somehow come to terms with the Church, and not vice versa.

How Catholic ecclesiology developed into a canonical, polemically oriented triumphalism is the object of concern in the next chapter.

Chapter 4

The Development of Church-Centered Theology

Strictly speaking, until about the year 1300 with the advent of Gallicanism, there was no theological treatise dealing expressly with the Church. However, we have already seen that the question of the Church is 'everywhere present in the New Testament even where it is not manifest in concepts and imagery' (Schnackenburg). And it is more than a probability that a biblical ecclesiology can be constructed. The same is generally true in the case of the immediately postbiblical period, the age of the great Fathers of the Church. The earliest controversies were concerned with Christology and the Trinity; ecclesiology was only indirectly at issue. Nevertheless, insofar as the Fathers addressed themselves to the problem of the Church, their fundamental orientation more closely approximated the biblical perspective than the scholastic theology that was to follow. The Fathers preserved the sense of mystery: the Church is the sacrament of Christ, his very presence in history. Bossuet summed up the entire patristic tradition when he described the Church as 'Jesus Christ spread abroad and communicated'.

'The thought of the Fathers,' M. J. LeGuillou writes, 'is completely dominated by the movement of revelation and of the economy of salvation, which begins in God and passes through Christ to the Church. Patristic thought sees all things in the light of revelation and of the saving action of God in Jesus Christ. It is thus that the Fathers speak of God, Christ, the Church, and the sacraments, as a dynamic and intimate unity. . . . God has also raised up the Church in the likeness of the Son, which having sprung forth from the action of the Word, and fulfilling itself through the sacraments, shows itself to be communion with Wisdom in the Holy Spirit, while awaiting the time of the full manifestation of glory.'[1]

Although one must be careful of any sweeping generalizations concerning patristic theology, it seems fair to suggest that the Fathers of the Church, by and large, emphasized the *identification* of Christ and the Church rather than their *differences*. For the Fathers, Christ is the Word and Wisdom of God manifesting himself in order that he might transform us into his glory. The beginning of this process occurs in the communion of the Church where the transforming revelation of the Mystery is accomplished. The Church, then, is seen as a part of God's plan of self-disclosure and his invitation to personal communion with him. It is the Body of Christ, the presence of the mystery of Christ, and the organism of its manifestation to the world.[2]

Since patristic theology was so thoroughly and so essentially biblical, this particular orientation is not difficult to understand. And until the twelfth century theology remained fundamentally and exclusively biblical. Indeed, theology was referred to as *sacra pagina* or *sacra scriptura*. But by the twelfth century theology came under the rule of dialectics (a foretaste, so to speak, of the contemporary flirtation with linguistic analysis). For Abelard, who typified so well the new theological mood, the function of theology was to show that the doctrinal propositions conform to the laws of predictability, i.e., to furnish a logical justification for the statements of faith. His famous work *Sic et Non* was an attempt to reconcile apparently opposed texts. With Abelard Christian theology passed from the *sacra pagina* to an embryonic systematics, and his influence on St Thomas Aquinas would prove to be considerable.

The twelfth century, too, marked the turning point for theological reflection on the Church. Thenceforth, two currents were preparing the way for a new form of ecclesiology: the antihierarchical spiritual movement and the communal movement. These gave rise, in turn, to Conciliarism and eventually the Reformation itself. Several key assumptions were challenged: the authority of the Pope, the reality of the Church as an institution for salvation, the place of authority, the ministerial priesthood, the necessity of sacraments, etc. The Church was reduced, so to speak, to the community which constitutes it. Until this time, a theology of the Church was more assumed than explicitly proposed. But in the heat of controversy and under the impact of dissent, theologians began addressing themselves directly to issues of ecclesiology. James of Viterbo's *De Regimine Christiano*, which appeared in 1301 or 1302, has been called the oldest treatise on the Church. A few months later there appeared Giles of Rome's *De Ecclesiastica Potestate* and John of Paris's *De Potestate Regia et Papali*. All three works were occasioned by the conflict between Philip the Fair and Boniface VIII. The titles of the books afford a clue to the new orientation of Catholic ecclesiological thought. All were concerned with questions of power and government, with the authority and rights of the Church. This was a reactionary theology in the strictest sense of the word: a reaction against contemporary challenges to the traditional institutional structures of the Church.

It was again a theology of papal power that had to be worked out against William of Ockham, Marsiglio of

Padua, and John of Janduno, and then against the proponents of the conciliarist theories. The talented men of this
time were mostly on the conciliarist side, but ability was not
totally absent from the so-called 'defenders of orthodoxy':
Thomas Netter, John of Ragusa, and John of Turrecremata.
The Protestant explosion only intensified the 'orthodox' bias
in favor of structures, juridical procedures, and institutional
realities. The delicate balance achieved by the great Fathers
of the Church was destroyed. Ecclesiology became apologetical, polemical, and canonical. Yves Congar has described
the phenomenon in this fashion:

> The treatise on the Church is a particular treatise composed
> in answer to Gallicanism, to conciliarism, to the purely
> spiritual ecclesiology of Wycliff and Hus, to Protestant
> negations, later on to those of secular 'stateism', Modern-
> ism, and so on. It follows that it is composed in reaction
> against errors all of which call the hierarchical structure of
> the Church in question. The *de Ecclesia* (tract) was princi-
> pally, sometimes almost exclusively, a defense and
> affirmation of the reality of the Church as machinery of
> hierarchical mediation, of the powers and primacy of the
> Roman see, in a word, a 'hierarchology'.[3]

The best symbol of the new 'hierarchology' is St Robert
Bellarmine (1542–1631) whose celebrated definition of the
Church in his book *De controversiis Christianae fidei adversus
nostri temporis haereticos* (1586) towers over the whole development: 'The one and true Church is the assembly of men,
bound together by the profession of the same Christian
faith, and by the communion of the same sacraments, under
the rule of legitimate pastors, and in particular of the one
vicar of Christ on earth, the Roman Pontiff.'[4] The definition
comprises three basic elements: (1) profession of the true
faith (which falls under the authority of the magisterium);

(2) communion of the same sacraments (which is embraced by the power of orders); and (3) submission to legitimate authority (which follows from the power of jurisdiction).

Consequently, it was relatively easy to exclude various people from true membership in the Church: (1) all non-Christians are out for lack of faith; (2) catechumens and excommunicated persons are out by reason of their exclusion, antecedent or consequent, from the sacraments; and (3) schismatics are out because of the rupture of union with the Pope. The characteristic note of Bellarmine's definition is its insistence on visibility. The outward profession of faith, communion of the sacraments, and adherence to legitimate ecclesiastical authority suffices. 'The Church is indeed a community [*coetus*] of men, as visible and palpable as the community of the Roman people, or the kingdom of France or the republic of Venice.' Bellarmine, of course, omits from his definition any idea that the union of Christians with Christ is a communion of life. He misses the whole point of St Paul's theology of the Body of Christ, and reduces the Pauline notion to a juridical or political metaphor.

Bellarmine's influence on subsequent ecclesiology should not be underestimated. His definition is attractively simple and canonically practical. He won over both dogmaticians and canon lawyers, and not a few catechism authors. And through his principal contemporary disciple, Sebastian Tromp, S.J., for the most part he also won over Pope Pius XII.[5]

With the Counter Reformation (typified by Bellarmine) the biblical-patristic synthesis is totally destroyed. Not only is the Church–Kingdom relationship completely ignored, but even the body-concept (which underlines the identity of Christ and Church) is twisted to serve the apologetical and canonical needs of the Church under siege. The Church is seen as the center of history and as the ordinary means of salvation for all mankind. This is what I have called the 'Ptolemaic' Church.

Tromp is absolutely faithful to the Counter Reformation tradition when he writes: 'Subjective redemption is brought about only by the Church, just as objective redemption is brought about on the cross.'[6] The purpose of all powers and functions within the Church is 'the increase of the Body of Christ'.[7] Indeed, the Church *is* the Kingdom of God on earth. 'The Father sends the Son, in order that the Son, through the Kingdom of God on earth, may bring all men to the Kingdom of God in heaven.'[8] Not only does Tromp illegitimately identify Church and Kingdom, but he also attempts to separate the Kingdom-on-earth from the Kingdom-in-heaven.

The business of the Church, according to Tromp, is purely external. Christ established a 'visible government that man might be called back to the things that are invisible'.[9] The primary aspect of Christ's founding of the Church is the institution of a sacred *magisterium*, to which he delivered the entire deposit of faith; a sacred *imperium*, to which he gave the basic law; and a sacred *ministerium*, to which he delivered the instruments of sanctification. Christ did this in order that his own threefold messianic mission might be continued.

And how does Tromp describe the mission of Christ? 'The Son is sent to the whole human race as the unique supreme teacher, teaching authoritively what he has heard from the Father; as the unique absolute legislator, promulgating laws by the Father's command; as the unique High-Priest, the mediator between the Father and men.'[10] Then he became 'the first visible Head of the Church', an office which he handed on to Peter and his successors after his own Ascension into heaven. 'The Church,' for Tromp, 'is the juridical and ethical continuation of the mission of Christ, in the manner of a true and perfect society, hierarchically constituted, universal and perpetual, equipped with various organs both for providing for its mission and for attaining the end proper to itself.'[11] And what is the Church's ultimate goal? It is the worship of God in the sanctification of men, terminating in the beatific vision. 'From the nature of the Church flow her inalienable properties: unity and uniqueness; visibility and recognizability; sanctity and credibility; immutability and indefectibility; the necessity of the Church for the attainment of salvation.'[12] Tromp carries his thought even further by embracing the opinion of Bellarmine that the whole Christian republic, including the civil power, is one Mystical Body. Indeed, 'a civil government which acknowledges the laws of the Catholic Church can be regarded as a special function in the Body of Christ'.[13]

Tromp laments the fact that his views on the theology of the Church have not always been accepted universally, even by his fellow Catholics. But he insists that, with the publication of the encyclical by Pope Pius XII (*Mystici Corporis*, 1943), there is no longer room for any debate. 'If a duly instructed Christian is asked what the earthly Church is, he will without doubt answer with one or another statement equivalent to the formula: the Church of Christ here on earth is that religious society founded by Christ, which, since the ascent of the Lord, has been subject to the Roman Pontiff.'[14] Tromp commends such an answer and urges that a similar response be given for the question, 'What is the Mystical Body of Christ?' It is none other than the Roman Catholic Church. 'It is called the *Body* of Christ because it is a visible organism, instituted by Christ and visibly directed by Christ in his visible Vicar. It is called the *Mystical* Body of Christ because by means of an invisible principle instilled in it by Christ, that is, by the Spirit of Christ Himself, that organization, in itself, in its organs, and in its members, is unified and quickened and united to Christ and brought to perfect likeness to Him.'[15]

The Church is a 'society of men in which some are placed over the others with full and perfect power to rule, to teach, and to judge. This society is therefore by its own force and nature unequal, i.e., it contains two orders of persons: the pastors, and the flock, i.e., on the one hand, those who have been placed in the various degrees of the hierarchy, on the other, the multitude of the faithful'.[16]

Pursuing this tradition, Tromp reiterates his conviction that 'whoever does not adhere to the Roman Pontiff, the Vicar of our Lord Jesus Christ, is not of the Catholic Church. . . . The Roman Pontiff is the bridegroom of the Church, by the power of the divine Bridegroom; he is the foundation, by the power of Christ the Foundation; he is the head, by the power of Christ the Head.'[17]

He concludes his full-length study of the Church with a final definition which exceeds two hundred words. It will suffice to quote only the first part of the definition because it embodies in a concise and starkly unambiguous fashion the theological tradition of Counter Reformation polemics (Bellarmine in particular), and it provides the proper theological context for a study of Pope Pius XII's encyclical on the Mystical Body, of which Father Tromp was the chief architect: 'The Mystical Body of Christ, precisely insofar as it is, and is rightly called "mystical", is that universal and social religious organization in which, by means of a juridical and visible mission, the magisterium, imperium and sacerdotium of Christ are continued under the one vicar of Christ, and in which the faithful, in accordance with the various states willed by Christ, collaborate with the hierarchy in extending the kingdom of Christ. . . .'[18]

The Church is primarily an hierarchically structured

institution which exists to save people. The most important people in the Church are the Pope and bishops (although it is not really clear how important the bishops are in relation to the Pope) because they, alone, have the special power from Christ to teach, to rule, and to sanctify. Anyone else who might share this power in the Church merely participates in or collaborates with the powers of the hierarchy. The Church is a visible society, which has all the qualities and resources of any given national state (no different, Bellarmine insisted, from the republic of Venice), and therefore should be expected to operate as political governments would operate: with its own ideology, court system, diplomatic corps, corridors of power, etc. And all of these prerogatives and privileges and rights are due the Church because of the mission which she has been given to perform: the continuation of the saving work of Christ, i.e., the teaching of hidden divine truths, the handing down of rules of life, and mediating in all spiritual matters between God and men. This is the 'Ptolemaic' Church in its fullest form. With only minor variation, *Mystici Corporis* endorsed it.[19]

Just prior to the appearance of the encyclical, a kind of neospiritualist movement or tendency developed in Germany whereby the visible and invisible elements in the Church were once again dichotomized at the expense of the hierarchical aspect. Various suggestions have been offered for this underground reaction to Mystical Body theology: the growth of the ecumenical movement, the new vigor of the biblical movement with its strong emphasis on the Kingdom of God, the pneumatic ecclesiology of the Orthodox, and even a certain Augustinianism in the writings of Johannes Adam Möhler and Mathias Scheeben, two of the leading theologians of the nineteenth century. A typical example of this new trend was Karl Pelz's *Der Christ als Christus* (1939) in which the union of Christ and the Christian was compared with transubstantiation in the Eucharist. After this work was placed on the Index of Forbidden Books, a reaction set in against the notion of the 'Mystical Body'. Theologians began to mistrust it and one in particular, M. D. Koster, warned against an ecclesiology which emphasizes the body-concept over against that of the People of God. The Body is but one of the biblical images of the Church. It is an expression which can never be the definition of the Church.[20]

But the work of Tromp (and to a far lesser extent, that of Emile Mersch, S.J.) prevailed. As we have already seen, Tromp defined 'Body' in a sociological and corporative sense against the new spiritualistic ecclesiology in Germany and he proceeded to identify this 'Body' strictly with the Roman Catholic Church. And this is the position adopted in *Mystici Corporis*: 'If we would define and describe this true Church of Jesus Christ—which is the One, Holy, Catholic, and Apostolic, Roman Church—we shall find no expression more noble, more sublime or more divine than the phrase which calls it "the Mystical Body of Christ".'[21] The identification is reaffirmed and made unmistakably clear in the Pope's later encyclical *Humani Generis* (1950) wherein he states that the Mystical Body of Christ and the Roman Catholic Church are one and the same reality (*unum idemque esse*).[22]

The immediate occasion for writing *Mystici Corporis* was to counteract certain 'grave errors' about the doctrine of the Body of Christ, both inside and outside the Catholic Church. These errors included a false rationalism, a popular naturalism which viewed the Church merely as a juridical and social union, and a false mysticism which attempted 'to eliminate the immovable frontier that separates creatures from their Creator'.[23] Within the main body of the encyclical, the Pope singles out for special censure the notion of the purely 'pneumatological' Church, on the one hand, and the aforementioned 'false mysticism' on the other:

> As our predecessor of happy memory, Leo XIII, in his Encyclical, *Satis Cognitum*, asserts: 'The Church is visible because she is a Body.' Hence, they err in a matter of divine truth, who imagine the Church to be invisible, intangible, as something merely 'pneumatological', as they say, by which many Christian communities, though they differ from each other in their profession of faith, are united by a bond that eludes the senses.[24]

> We deplore and condemn the pernicious error of those who arbitrarily conceive of an imaginary Church, a kind of society that finds its origin and growth in charity, to which they somewhat contemptuously oppose another, which they call juridical. But this distinction, which they introduce, is baseless.[25]

The Pope's condemnation of 'false mysticism' is even more to the point of the exegetical development that was traced earlier in the third chapter:

> For there are some who neglect the fact that the Apostle Paul had used metaphorical language in speaking of this doctrine, and failing to distinguish the physical from the social Body of Christ as they should, arbitrarily draw some deformed kind of unity. They want the divine Redeemer and the members of the Church to coalesce into one physical person and while they bestow divine attributes on man, they make Christ our Lord subject to error and to human inclination towards evil.[26]

In an attempt to refute these errors the Pope develops his

teaching on the Mystical Body of Christ according to the tradition of the Latin Church which viewed the *soma Christou* in a corporative, collective sense, and also according to the predominant Catholic exegesis of his time. The encyclical makes many footnote references to the work of St Augustine and St Thomas Aquinas and only occasionally to St Robert Bellarmine. But mathematics can be misleading. The guiding spirit is Bellarmine and the guiding hand is Sebastian Tromp.

For *Mystici Corporis* the Church is a 'Body' in a way analogous to the human body.[27] The Church is the Body of *Christ* because 'our Lord is the Founder, the Head, the Support, and the Savior of this Mystical Body'.[28] The interpretation of the key text, I Cor 12:13, is clearly corporative.[29] Indeed, the corporative understanding of the Body of Christ is the foundation for all of the encyclical's theology: our spiritual dependence upon Christ,[30] the 'Christusmythik' of the exegetes,[31] the 'gratia capitis' of the Scholastics,[32] the theology of the sacraments,[33] and the theology of the Holy Spirit.[34]

Herein, therefore, we have a general reaffirmation of the 'Ptolemaic' ecclesiology of the Counter Reformation period. The Church exists as the ordinary means of salvation. Although Christ could have imparted the graces of salvation immediately, 'He wished to do so only through a visible Church that would be formed by the union of men, and thus through the Church every man would perform a work of collaboration with Him in dispensing the graces of Redemption. The Word of God willed to make use of our nature, when in excruciating agony he would redeem mankind; in much the same way throughout the centuries he makes use of the Church that the work begun might endure.'[35]

The Pope, through his Holy Office, reaffirmed this

'Ptolemaic' ecclesiology in the letter to Cardinal Cushing of Boston (August 9, 1949) regarding the views of Fr Leonard Feeney, S.J., on the problem of salvation outside the Church. Father Feeney had merely drawn the scholastic ecclesiology to its logical conclusions, insisting that if salvation is possible only within the Roman Catholic Church, then those outside the Church are necessarily damned. The Holy Office, operating as always with the context of Father Tromp's ecclesiology, proposed the distinction between *in re* and *in voto* membership: 'To gain eternal salvation it is not always required that a person be incorporated *in fact* as a member of the Church, but it is required that he belong to it in *desire* and *longing*.' And this 'desire' can even be implicit, when a man simply wishes to act in accord with the will of God. Citing *Mystici Corporis*, the document states: 'Only those are *really* to be included as members of the Church who have been baptized and profess the true faith, and who have not had the misfortune of withdrawing from the body or for grave faults been cut off by legitimate authority.' Those others who are not really members of the Catholic Church can, indeed, be saved, but 'they cannot be secure about their salvation . . . since they lack many great gifts and helps from God, gifts they can enjoy only in the Catholic Church.'[36]

It is the central argument of this book that this theology of the Church is radically distorted and that the distortion arises from the failure to discern the Church in its proper relation to the Kingdom of God. What is demanded in our time is a recognition, in the first instance, of the inadequacy and even inaccuracy of this earlier theology, and the launching of a Copernican Revolution which will place the Church where it belongs, as both sign and instrument of the Kingdom of God, but always subordinate to it. It is the Kingdom and not the Church which is the center of salvation history. The Church is the extraordinary, not the ordinary means of salvation.

Functionalist, mission-centered ecclesiology must come to terms with the compelling data of both the New Testament and the early Fathers of the Church that the Church is more than the sum total of its membership; that it is, in some distinctive way, the very presence of Christ in history. This means that the functionalist must be prepared to reflect more thoroughly and more carefully on the 'mysterious' character of the Church and on its unique relationship with Christ himself. What does it mean to say that the Church is the very Body of Christ? If it is less than the Body of Christ, what, then, *is* the Church? And if it is *much* less than the Body of Christ, of what theological significance is its mission? Why should there be a Church at all? Is it simply the corpse of God, or his grave? But I must hasten to add that I do not have *Mystici Corporis* ecclesiology in mind when I urge a reconsideration of the Pauline and patristic notions of the Body of Christ. This theology is still too juridical, too narcissistic, and in a word, Ptolemaic. It is the Body of Christ as proposed by the newer exegesis and as endorsed by theologians with such ironclad functionalist credentials as Dietrich Bonhoeffer and Bishop John Robinson, that I am thinking of.

So, too, must the 'High-Church' theologians be called to an accounting. It is no longer sufficient to extoll the Church as the sacrament of Christ or the People of God or to employ any other biblical or patristic image that might attract our attention and support. This still assumes too much. Is the Church, in fact, meant to be the center of history? Is it, indeed, the ordinary means of salvation? Does it make sense theologically to divide the world into three large camps: explicit members of the Church, members by desire, and the damned? Is the Church the touchstone of proximity to the Lord? Did Christ's mission concentrate exclusively or even primarily on the establishment of a Church that would, as is said, 'carry on his work?' Even the Second Vatican Council indicates in that key fifth article of *Lumen Gentium* that Christ came to proclaim and to establish the Kingdom. And no biblical scholar or theologian of any serious competence would suggest today that the Kingdom which he had in mind is none other than the Christian Church.

No, it is the Kingdom and not the Church which is at the heart of the preaching of Jesus and at the core of his entire ministry. He came that men might see in him the reality of life and the meaning of all history. He came to demonstrate that the way of love, of mutual concern, of compassion, of generosity, of sensitivity, is the only truly *human* way, and that to choose otherwise, to choose self-interest over the interest of others, to follow the path of exploitation rather than reconciliation, is to choose the path of failure for all life and for all history. This is what the Kingdom of God is all about. To the extent that men are reconciled one to another in Christ, the Kingdom is in process. The Church exists to proclaim the rightness of this process, to cooperate in its realization here and now, and to offer itself as a model of genuine human community. The Church presumes to do this, not out of a spirit of extraordinary arrogance, but out of the conviction that by the election and grace of God she has been transformed into the very Body of Christ and that she has, thereby, the same explicit responsibility for the Kingdom of God that Jesus had.

From the twelfth century on (and some would argue that the decisive moment occurred in 313 when the Church accepted, via the Edict of Milan, the privileges and prerogatives of political approbation and preferment)[37] Christian theology began to go off course in its systematic reflections on the Church. The 'death-of-God' Protestant position on the left and the Bellarmine-Tromp position on the right are evidence of a radical disturbance somewhere underneath. The latter extreme fashioned and sustained the Ptolemaic Church, the former extreme ridicules and rejects it—not only the adjective but also the noun. This is not to suggest that all defects lie on the extremities of the theological spectrum. Left of center, but hardly extreme, lies the position of a Harvey Cox; right of center, and hardly extreme, lies the position of many reputable Catholic theologians.[38] No theologian has yet worked out a systematic theology of the Church which preserves a proper balance between the Church as the Body of Christ and the Church as sign and instrument of the Kingdom of God. Bishop Robinson has made a good beginning, although much of his ecclesiology has to be systematized from without. He has never produced a consciously systematic theology of the Church. Furthermore, if he had the time and the inclination to produce such an ecclesiology, it is clear in what direction it would proceed: 'The doctrine of the Church has never consistently been worked out from the end of the Kingdom: the Kingdom has regularly been seen from the end of the Church.'[39]

In any case, with the appearance of *Mystici Corporis* Catholic ecclesiology reached the end of the Ptolemaic path. What more could be said? We had produced a theology with an element of biblical and patristic flavor, and with a minor bow to the Pauline notion of the Body of Christ, but the major assumption remained untouched: the Church is a hierarchically structured institution, founded by Christ to communicate the fruits of the redemption to all mankind. The Church exists to save people, and it is the normal or ordinary means of their salvation. It is Christ's very Body, and as such it is at the center of everything. All men must come to terms with it. The Church is God's agent in the world, and the world's only real hope of 'getting to God'.

As indicated in the first chapter, the actual situation in the post–*Mystici Corporis* world radically undercut the easy assumptions of this kind of ecclesiology. The Church was a minority in the world, and becoming increasingly more of a minority. Is there any real point to insisting that the Church is, regardless of the facts to the contrary, the ordinary means of salvation? And in the light of industrialization and urbanization, the rapid advances in technology, the population explosion, the growing internationalization of politics, economics, and culture, people have begun to wonder why we need a Church at all, and particularly a Church which, they feel, makes such pretentious claims and offers such poor performance. People began considering the 'death-of-God' only after they were ready to give up on the Church.

The theological tide has only just begun to change. Catholic ecclesiology is moving almost imperceptibly away from and beyond the conventional wisdom of Bellarmine, Tromp, and the encyclical of Pius XII. There is some little evidence of this in the documents of the Second Vatican Council, some slight recognition that the mere repetition of the Ptolemaic thesis will not change the facts as they really are. How far Vatican II has brought us will be the concern of Part III.

Part Three

THE THEOLOGY
OF THE CHURCH
AT THE SECOND VATICAN
COUNCIL

Chapter 5

Advances in the Theology of the Church

Almost all of the sixteen documents and decrees of the Second Vatican Council are concerned with ecclesiology, with the question of the Church as such. Indeed, when Pope Paul VI addressed the bishops at the opening of the second session of the council, just three months after his own election, he reviewed the 'main objectives' of Vatican II: 'the knowledge, or . . . the awareness of the Church; its reform; the bringing together of all Christians in unity; the dialogue of the Church with the contemporary world'. The central question of the Second Vatican Council was clearly the question of the Church.

The principal texts for the council's developing ecclesiology are the *Dogmatic Constitution on the Church (Lumen Gentium)*, the *Pastoral Constitution on the Church in the Modern World*, the *Decree on Ecumenism*, and the *Constitution on the Sacred Liturgy*. These provide the larger theological context within which all the other decrees make sense (e.g., the decrees on priestly training and life, on bishops, on the missions, on the laity, on religious liberty, etc.). And of these four major ecclesiological documents, the *Dogmatic Constitution on the Church* holds the place of honor, a kind of *primus inter pares*. Accordingly, rather than convert the next two chapters into a running commentary on the various key documents of the council,[1] I shall confine my remarks to *Lumen Gentium* and, more specifically still, to the first chapter of the Constitution, 'The Mystery of the Church.'[2] In this chapter alone, we can see the agonizing transition from the purely Ptolemaic ecclesiology of the Bellarmine–Tromp axis to the Copernican and post-Copernican ecclesiologies of the contemporary scene. It will be argued herein that the ecclesiology of Vatican II is lodged somewhere between the Ptolemaic and the Copernican churches. Insofar as it has moved beyond the former, it represents a welcome advance and bears the seeds of hope for the future; and to the extent that it is still distant from the latter, it merits a genuinely frank, critical response.

What should be clear at the outset is that the overwhelming majority of the bishops at the Second Vatican Council rejected much of the Bellarmine–Tromp theology of the Church, even though most Catholics had been led to believe that this earlier ecclesiology was simply the common belief of the Church and the unanimous view of theologians—at least of 'orthodox' theologians. The work of the Council rendered this assumption implausible. As I have already indicated in Part II, preconciliar seminary theology proposed the Church as an hierarchically structured organization which exists to save people. The Church is an institution before it is a community. The fullness of authority in this institution resides in the Pope, and so questions of papal primacy and Petrine succession occupied much space and attention in these earlier discussions on the Church. The problem of the Magisterium of the Church usually followed at this point. It would be shown how this authority resides in the Pope and in the bishops and in what sense and under what conditions their teaching might be infallible (i.e., free from all doctrinal error). The notion of the Church as the Body of Christ would have occupied about a paragraph in some of these manuals and textbooks of theology, but in the wake of Pope Pius XII's encyclical letter on the Mystical Body, the attention of theologians turned to this particular image of the Church. Even so, as we have seen, the juridical and hierarchical aspect of the Church maintained its place of eminence in the discussion.

The starting point of the ecclesiology of Vatican II is strikingly different. The Church is a *mystery* before it is an institution or an organization. It is a mystery because it is the presence of the merciful Lord among men. Therefore, it is a mystery even in its institutional and juridical structure. The Church is also the *sacrament* of Christ, the visible presence of Christ in the world. And it is a *pilgrim community*, or the People of God, with a mission within as well as beyond the confines of history. Indeed, the Church cannot be viewed apart from history. What should also be clear is that the perspective of the Constitution is neither apologetical nor defensive. It does not attempt at the start to prove that the Church is a divinely established institution with a teaching authority whose origin can be traced back to the apostles. The Magisterium is set in a larger context and it is fully intelligible only within this larger context.

The Church as the Sacrament of Christ

The first paragraph of the *Constitution on the Church* speaks of the Church as being 'in Christ like a sacrament or sign and instrument of a very closely knit union with God and of the unity of the whole human race'. The Church is the sacrament of Christ.

The notion of sacrament (i.e., a visible sign of some invisible reality) is fundamental to an understanding of religion in general and the Christian life in particular. All religious activity is designed to achieve some kind of union between the divine and the human. Whatever means (symbols, gestures, rites) are employed for this purpose have a 'sacramental' character. They are external signs by which God encounters man, and man encounters God. Direct contact through mystical experience is not the normal manner of divine-human encounter. The human condition, limited as it is to the material order (but I do not use the word 'limited' in any kind of Platonic, antisecular sense), demands some form of outward, visible expression of the mysterious, invisible, holy reality. The transcendental is meaningless if it cannot be encountered at some concrete point.

The transcendental has intervened decisively in our history in the person and ministry of Jesus Christ. The sacramental life of the Church exists to dramatize publicly and symbolically what has already taken place in history, what is about to occur in the future, and what is actually happening here and now. God is taking hold of all his creation through the mediation of his Son. And the power and foundation of the Son's word and work is in the Holy Spirit.

Christ is preeminently the sacrament of God because, in his single personality, there resides the fullness of God and the completeness of man. He is the most effective sign of God's merciful love, 'for it is in Christ that the complete being of the Godhead dwells embodied, and in him you have been brought to completion' (Col 2:9). And from our side, he is the perfect response to the Father's merciful love. He is one with us, the one mediator between God and man. 'Through him God chose to reconcile the whole universe to himself, making peace through the shedding of his blood upon the cross—to reconcile all things, whether on earth or in heaven, through him alone' (Col 1:20; see also 1 Tim 2:5).

Jesus Christ, therefore, is the sacrament of our encounter with God. He is the visible expression of the merciful love of God and of our own human response to that love. Christ is that unique point where divine initiative and human responsibility meet. If we speak of Christ as the sacrament of God, as that point of encounter between God and man in the here and now, then we are speaking of the Risen Lord. Our contact is not with the Jesus of Good Friday but with the Christ of Easter Sunday. The problem is not: how do we span twenty centuries and so restore contact with Jesus as he strolls through the hillsides of Palestine or as he hangs dying on the cross. Our encounter is with the Christ of today, the Lord who sits at the right hand of the Father interceding for us—even now (Heb 11:24 ff.). It is the Christ who continues his mission of worship and suffering service.

But where do we encounter the Risen Christ? The same sacramental principle is to be applied. Just as Christ is the sacrament of God, so the Church is the sacrament of the Risen Christ. The Church is the visible, outward sign of the redemptive love and mercy of the Father in Christ. And the Church is the place where man responds—through word, work, and worship—to the divine initiative in Christ. 'The Church, therefore, is not merely a means of salvation,' Edward Schillebeeckx, O.P., writes in his classic work, *Christ the Sacrament of Encounter with God*,[3] 'it is Christ's salvation itself, this salvation as visibly realized in this world.' Indeed, the Church is the Body of the Risen Lord.

Given this larger sacramental context (namely, that Christ is the sacrament of God, and the Church the sacrament of Christ), we should be able to see that the seven sacraments are essentially acts of Christ in his Church. They are signs of faith as well as causes of grace. But they are preeminently privileged points of encounter with the Risen Lord.[4]

To designate the Church as the sacrament of Christ is no idle gesture. It provides us with a view of the mystery of the Church which a lifetime of theologizing and reflection cannot hope to exhaust. It also poses for the Church a sharp-edged challenge. If, indeed, the Church is the Body of the

Risen Lord and the sacrament of his presence in the world, then the Church's task is to demonstrate this reality to the world in a convincing manner. The Church is the sacrament of Christ, but if the Church does not live as Christ, then the sign is pointing to a nonexistent reality—in which case the sacrament is a lie. The present renewal of the Church has but one basic goal: to renew the face of the Church in the image and likeness of her Risen Lord.

The Mystery of the Church

Social agencies, on the local, national, or international level (e.g., the Peace Corps), do the work of Christ insofar as they minister to mankind in his needs, bind up his wounds in the spirit of the Good Samaritan, and restore to men their sense of human dignity. The Church must have this same passion for social justice and this same sensitive concern for the divisions and inequities in our society. But the Church is not simply one of many social agencies—the one which happens to be the largest and most international in character. The Church is a mystery, 'a people made one with the unity of the Father, the Son and the Holy Spirit' (*Constitution on the Church*, art. 4).

The term 'mystery' does not refer to an unsolved crime or to truths which cannot be understood by the power of reason alone. It is St Paul who provides us with the fundamental theological meaning of 'mystery', identifying it with the will and purpose of God which has been 'set forth in Christ, as a plan for the fullness of time, to unite all things in him, things in heaven and things on earth' (Eph 1:9–10). And later in the same epistle, St Paul includes the Church in the total notion of mystery (Eph 5:32).[5]

To refer to the Church as a mystery is to say, at the very

least, that there is more to the Church than meets the eye, that the essential reality of the Church is not exhausted by its external, visible, and human structure. The Church is something more than a religious *organization*; it is an *organism*, the very Body of Christ. The Church is, in the words of Karl Rahner, 'The official presence of the grace of Christ in the public history of the one human race.' The council endorses this view in its *Decree on the Missions* as well (art. 9): the Church is 'nothing else and nothing less than a manifestation or epiphany of God's will, and the fulfillment of that will in world history'.

The Church is a mystery, therefore, because it is the embodiment of God's plan for his people. But the heart and concrete expression of that plan is Christ, and the Church is the Body of Christ. Consequently, the mystery of the Church cannot be viewed apart from the plan of God and its execution and fulfillment in the course of human history. And this is the starting point for the discussion of the Church by the council. This orientation is especially clear in that key first chapter of *Lumen Gentium*.

The Eternal Father's *plan* was 'to raise men to a participation of the divine life' (art. 2). The Father patterned this plan after the image of Christ, 'the first born among many brethren' (Rom 8:29). Furthermore, the Father 'planned to assemble in the holy Church all those who would believe in Christ'. The unfolding of the Father's plan took place at the dawn of history and within history itself, and particularly during the period of the Old Covenant with Israel, and in the present era with the outpouring of the Holy Spirit. 'At the end of time it will gloriously achieve completion, when . . . all the just . . . will be gathered together with the Father in the universal Church.' The Father's plan is realized in and through Christ, for Christ is the sacrament of our encounter with God. In Christ, we have been chosen and predestined to become adopted sons of the Father. It is the will of the Father that all things be reestablished in Christ (Eph 1:10). All men are called to union with Christ, to work for the coming of the Kingdom.

The Church is the sign of our unity in Christ. It is the 'first fruits' of the final destiny of all mankind. Indeed, the Church is that relatively tiny segment of mankind which publicly acknowledges the Lordship of Christ, which gives visible and deliberate witness to its faith in Christ as the ultimate meaning and director of all history (see art. 3). The power of Christ's work resides in the Holy Spirit. Not until Jesus died on the cross and rose from the dead was he empowered to send forth the Spirit (see Acts 2:32–33). Since Pentecost, the Holy Spirit dwells in the Church as in a temple (1 Cor 3:16; 6:19); the Spirit guides, unifies, and vivifies the Church. It is the Spirit which moves the Church to say to Jesus, the Lord: 'Come!' (Apoc 22:17; see *Lumen Gentium*, art. 4).

The Church is a mystery because it is the social and historical embodiment of God's plan for mankind: the merciful plan of the Father to gather all men into a single family. The Father chooses to encounter us and wills that we encounter him in and through his Son, Jesus Christ. The Church is the central point of that encounter, because she is the Body of Christ. The mission of this community, which is the Body of the Lord, is to unify mankind, to gather together, to bind up wounds, to reconcile, to heal, to save that which is lost. The principle of unity, both within and outside of the Church, is the Holy Spirit—the Spirit of love and of life.

This is the place where Vatican II began to construct its own theology of the Church. For the council, the Church is neither an international social agency nor a religious organization in which the most important elements are the laws and the bylaws, and the most important people the officers and administrators. Liberal Protestantism of the early twentieth century and some functionalist ecclesiologies of the present time have begun at the former point, and some Catholic theology of these same periods has begun at the latter point. Both are theological blind alleys.

The Church and the Kingdom of God

I have already referred to article 5 of *Lumen Gentium* in the preceding chapter. The document recalls that the Kingdom of God was at the heart of the preaching and ministry of Jesus and that it manifested itself in his word, in his work, and in his very person. The Church has received the mission to 'proclaim and to establish among all peoples the Kingdom of Christ and of God and makes up the germ and the beginning of that Kingdom on earth'. According to Canon Charles Moeller, professor of theology at the University of Louvain, an official of the Vatican Congregation for the Doctrine of the Faith, and one of the original authors of *Lumen Gentium*, this fifth article was inserted at a later stage of the Constitution's development to counteract the complaint of 'triumphalism'. 'The insertion of a section devoted to the Kingdom of God cut short the temptation to identify the Church in its present state with the Kingdom of God.'[6]

In Part II I insisted that reflection on the body-image underlines the identification of Christ and the Church, while reflection on the Church–Kingdom relationship underlines the dichotomy between Church and Christ. But this is not a hard and fast rule. 'No less serious than to identify Church and Kingdom of God,' Rudolf Schnackenburg writes, 'would be to weaken or destroy the relationship of the Church to the future Kingdom of God.'[7] For the Church is filled even now with the 'powers of the age to come'.

When Simon Peter receives the 'keys of the Kingdom of heaven' (Mt 16:19), he is given the function and authority to provide access to the Kingdom of God to the candidates for salvation who gather in the Church. Even the Protestant theologian Oscar Cullmann indicates that Peter 'is to lead the people of God into the resurrection Kingdom'.[8]

To fulfill this function, divine authority is needed which Jesus himself exercised during his own public ministry, and, in particular, the authority to forgive sins (see Mk 2:10). And so the power of binding and loosing has been conferred on Peter and the other apostles (Mt 18:18). The scope of this power of binding and loosing extended fundamentally as far as Jesus' authority on earth extended, and thereby comprised the power of forgiving sins (see also Jn 20:23), authoritative teaching (Mk 1:22, 27), and the power over the devils (see Mk 3:15; 6:7). 'Precisely this last,' Schnackenburg writes, 'shows the deepest meaning of all Jesus' authority (see also Mk 11:28 f., 33 parallels): to break the rule of Satan (see Lk 11:20; Mt 12:28) and to establish the reign of God.'[9]

Despite the fact that failure and sin will continue to exist even within the Church, this Christian community shall perdure until the end of time for the Risen Lord is within it. And this orientation of the Church toward the future Kingdom is most dramatically and symbolically revealed in the central act of worship, the Eucharist. For this is the celebration of the New Covenant in the blood of Jesus, and this New Covenant has established the Kingdom of God among men and insures the coming of the perfect Kingdom at the end of history. The common celebration of the Eucharist is the sign, the ritual anticipation, and the sacramental preparation for the 'eating and drinking at Jesus' table in his Kingdom' (see Lk 22:30). 'For as often as you shall eat this bread and drink the chalice of the Lord, you shall announce the death of the Lord until he comes' (1 Cor 11:26).

This key Pauline description of the Eucharist splendidly sets the Christian community in its proper historical and theological context. For the Church carries on her work 'between-the-times': between the 'already' of the death and Resurrection and the 'not yet' of the Second Coming of the Lord. The Eucharistic celebration is rooted in the saving events of the Lord's earthly ministry and looks toward the final perfection of all things in him (see Eph 1:9–10). 'Without exaggeration,' Schnackenburg writes, 'we may say that Jesus' institution at the Last Supper is one of the principal bases of this awareness of the early Church, the bridge that links Jesus' company of disciples and the Christian community after Easter, and an ever-flowing fountain for the interior life of God's people of the New Testament.'[10]

As such the Eucharistic assembly is a pledge of the coming Kingdom because it is, here and now, a sign of the present growth of the Kingdom. For the Kingdom of God comes into being wherever men accept one another as Christ accepted us, wherever men bear one another's burdens as Christ bore ours. The Eucharistic community, therefore, is a sign to the world that the building up of the community of mankind is the raw material of the Kingdom. The Church invites the world, so to speak, to look to her Eucharistic assemblies and to see the final destiny of all mankind foreshadowed therein.

In the end, the Eucharist is to be the pattern and ideal for the life of the Church as a community. The Church will be an effective (i.e., credible) sign of the Kingdom if she lives a Eucharistic life, which is a life of solidarity and fellowship (*koinonia*), of healing and of service (*diakonia*). Neither of these qualities excludes the institutional framework of the Church. In the Eucharistic assembly there is institutional order, for the liturgy itself is sacramentally and hierarchically structured. It is the bishop who is the high priest of the worshiping community (see the *Constitution on the Sacred Liturgy*, arts. 41–42), and his priests preside at the Eucharist in his name. With him and under his authority, they break the Bread of Life in word and in sacrament. And the liturgical renewal has reminded us that the Eucharist is not a clerical preserve, that each Christian participates according to his own place and function. This distribution of roles, under the headship of the one presiding at the Eucharist, reflects in its own way the ordered, institutional character of the Christian life.

It should be noted, if only parenthetically, that the council does not completely avoid the temptation of a clericalized understanding of the Eucharist. 'Though they differ from one another in essence and not only in degree,' the *Constitution on the Church* insists (art. 10), 'the common priesthood of the faithful and the ministerial or hierarchical priesthood are nonetheless inter-related: each of them in its own special way is a participation in the one priesthood of Christ.' On the one hand, the council admits that both the ordained and the nonordained participate in the one priesthood of Christ. On the other hand, it attempts to erect an essential distinction between them. However, the word 'priest' is not applied initially to Jesus or to his apostles. It is only later in the New Testament that the early Church referred to him as 'priest' (see especially the Epistle to the Hebrews), and then, too, the entire Christian community was described as priestly (1 Pet 2:5; Apoc 1:6, 5:10–25). In the second century the term 'priest' was applied to ordained ministers, and until the sixth century priesthood was conferred by a mere imposition of hands. Anointing with oil, which seemed to signify a special setting apart, did not begin until this time. So we must insist here, that, despite the importance of the distribution of roles in the Eucharistic liturgy, the priesthood of Christ overflows into the entire Church corporately—that is, the Church is itself a priestly community.[11]

The Church at worship (particularly in her Eucharistic assemblies) and the Church at work in the world (cooperating with men in the building up of the community of mankind) is to be the sign of the present Kingdom as well as the pledge of Christ's final victory at the end of history. But the Church also has a prophetic responsibility to be the sign of the *future* Kingdom, to remind the world that its designs cannot achieve perfection within the confines of human history, that it is not within the power and capacities of man to build the complete City of Man. The Lord alone can bring unity to mankind. He alone can gather all things under his headship. He alone can hand over the perfected creation to the Father (see Eph 1:10 and Col 1:20). And because the Church's faith includes this spirit of caution and reserve about the present accomplishments of man and the contemporary realization of the Kingdom of God, she must be prepared to criticize, to expose deficiencies, to exhort to repentance, and so forth. The Church gives witness to the future character of the Kingdom of God by stripping man of his illusions, his pretense, and his arrogance. And she must demonstrate, by the quality and character of her own life, that she has not thrown in her lot completely with the forces of this world. Her own spirit of detachment, of poverty, of unassuming suffering service will make her prophecy believable.

In summary, the Church has at least a threefold mission: to announce the Kingdom of God, to work here and now to bring it about, and to show by the quality and character of her own life as a community what the Kingdom is all about and what is to be the final destiny of mankind and of all history. Because the Kingdom of God has both a present and a future dimension, the Church must consciously strive to become an effective sign and instrument of the Kingdom in *both* its present and future aspects. She is a sign of the Kingdom in its present reality by working here and now for the healing of the divisions within the family of mankind, by ministering to man in his needs. And she is a sign of the present Kingdom in her Eucharistic life, by demonstrating the solidarity and fellowship of life in Christ. The Church is also a sign of the future Kingdom by refusing to embrace without qualification the standards and values of this world, for much of this world's activity is contrary to the spirit of the Gospel. By her prophetic chastisement, exhortation, and call to repentance, the Church gives witness to her belief that the Kingdom of God will be brought to perfection beyond our history and only by the initiative of the Lord.

'In a world that has become, or has become again, purely "worldly",' Yves Congar, O.P. has written, 'the Church finds herself forced, if she would still be anything at all, to be simply the Church, witness to the Gospel and the Kingdom of God, through Jesus Christ and in view of him. That is what men need, this is what they expect of her ... that she be simply the Church of Jesus Christ, the conscience of men in the light of the Gospel, but that she be this with her whole heart.'[12]

Biblical Images of the Church

Article 6 of *Lumen Gentium* indicates that 'the inner nature of the Church is now made known to us in different (biblical) images'. These are often taken from agriculture, architecture, and family life. Accordingly, the Church of the New Testament is variously described as a sheepfold, the field of God, a building, a holy temple, our mother, the Spouse of

Christ, and the Body of Christ. These biblical images are so diverse and, at times, seemingly contradictory that it is impossible to construct an adequate theology of the Church on the basis of any single image—even the Body of Christ. 'All these metaphors . . . ultimately remain insufficient and cannot adequately represent the unity and tension of the Church's existence which comprises earth and heaven, eschatological present and the future; precisely the inexpressibility points to the unfathomable mystery of the Church in the world between time and eternity.'[13]

The Church as a Sheepfold

The first of the biblical images of the Church to which the Second Vatican Council refers is that of the sheepfold: 'The Church is a *sheepfold* whose one and necessary door is Christ (Jn 10:1-10). It is a flock of which God himself foretold he would be the shepherd (cf. Is 40:11; Ezra 34:11 ff.), and whose sheep, although tended by human shepherds, are nevertheless ceaselessly led and nourished by Christ himself, the good shepherd, and the prince of the shepherds (cf. Jn 10:11; 1 Pet 5:4), who gave his life for the sheep (cf. Jn 10:11-16).'

By itself, the ecclesial image of the *sheepfold* labors under the same difficulties as that of *mother*. If the Church is to be described uncritically as our mother, the proper response of each member is one of dutiful and loving obedience. The relationship is one of dependence and submission. But membership in the Church is not exclusively analogous to the condition of children in a family. It is more precisely and more properly a fraternal relationship, and authority is exercised not so much in a parental fashion as in a fraternal, collegial manner. So, too, if the Church is simply analogous with a flock of sheep, there is little room for initiative and for a free, mature response to the call of God in history. The idea of community at work in history, shaping history's course and direction, as the *avant-garde* of God's Kingdom, is not easily extracted from the agrarian description of the Church as a 'sheepfold'.

Nevertheless, even this pastoral image has some immediate relevance in our own time—an age of urbanization and industrialization. For the Church is perennially the community which must give itself without measure to the building of the Kingdom of God. It is called out of its protected sanctuaries to be the public sign and instrument of the Kingdom, to profess its faith in the Lordship of Christ, and to demonstrate the meaning of life in Christ.

The shepherd-flock image of the Church serves as a useful qualification of the central christological title, 'Suffering Servant of God.' Jesus did not lay down his life reluctantly or under compulsion. He did not regard his mission simply as the fulfilling of a duty imposed upon him by his Father, as if he were merely following a Puritan ethic of responsibility. He gave himself up willingly, out of a spirit of compassion and mercy. At the time of the multiplication of the loaves, Jesus 'saw a large crowd, and had compassion on them, because they were like sheep without a shepherd' (Mk 6:34). And in the very act of crucifixion by which Jesus fulfilled the role of the Suffering Servant of God, he identified himself with the Good Shepherd who lays down his life for his sheep. He did this willingly and without complaint because he knew and loved his sheep, and his love went out beyond Israel to the Gentiles (see Jn 10:11–18).

The early Church seems to have recognized this intimate connection between the servant and shepherd ideas. Thus, in 1 Pet 5:1–4: 'Now I exhort the presbyters among you . . . tend the flock of God which is among you, governing not under constraint, but willingly, according to God; nor yet for the sake of base gain, but eagerly; nor yet as lording it over your charges, but becoming from the heart a pattern to the flock. And when the Prince of Shepherds appears, you will receive the unfading crown of glory.'

Reflection on the biblical concept of the Good Shepherd should help to purify and deepen our understanding of the Church's mission and of ecclesiastical authority. The Church is to be a servant Church, but she cannot exercise this ministry of suffering service begrudgingly or puritanically. She will not faithfully represent the Good Shepherd if she brings her healing powers to bear only after she has been compelled to do so by force of circumstances. The Servant Church is also a Shepherd Church—a community which is always prepared to lay down its life for its flock (and this flock is the entire body of mankind). The Church, like the Good Shepherd, has compassion on the multitude. She does not stop to count the cost. She gives herself willingly and not under constraint; eagerly, and not for base gain; not projecting herself to the forefront, but simply providing 'from the heart a pattern to the flock'. For the determining feature of the Good Shepherd is that he lays down his life for his sheep.

On the level of pastoral authority in the Church, it may demand the retirement from office, the relinquishing of administrative responsibility—for the sake of the sheep. When the pastor can no longer provide adequate service for his flock, he empties himself to the dregs for their sake. Any other course of action is to regard the sheepfold as a fief rather than a flock. And at the higher level of the Church's mission, it may mean the yielding of special economic privilege (tax-exempt status, for example) which, ironically, places a heavier burden on those whom the Church exists to serve.

The Shepherd Church must empty herself again and again. She lays down her life for her sheep that she might, in turn, be 'a pattern to the flock'. Paul-Émile Cardinal Léger's decision to retire as archbishop of Montreal to work among the lepers in Africa dramatizes more effectively than any theological argumentation what this biblical image is all about.

The Church as Temple

'God's whole purpose,' writes Yves Congar, O.P., 'is to make the human race, created in his image, a living, spiritual temple in which he not only dwells but to which he communicates himself and in turn receives from it the worship of a wholly filial obedience.'[14] The ultimate goal is that he will be 'all in all' (1 Cor 15:18).

God realizes his presence historically and in stages. His presence is manifested initially in creation itself—in the temple of nature. Methodically, he sets aside Israel as his chosen people and intervenes unexpectedly in its life as a nation and in the individual lives of the patriarchs. Then as soon as he forms this people as his own, he begins to exist *for* Israel, as her own particular God. He establishes his presence among them as one who reveals, judges, listens, asserts, directs, or punishes. But contrary to the perennial temptation of the Israelites, God's presence among his people could not be localized or materialized. The whole Old Testament offers a consistently condemnatory witness against this Israelite tendency to idolatry, i.e., the identification of God with this place or that place, with this object or that object.

After David had established his own royal palace in Jerusalem, the idea came to him to build a temple for Yahweh: 'See now, I dwell in a house of cedar, but the ark of God dwells in a tent' (2 Sam 7:2). But the prophet Nathan intervenes. While Nathan's remarks are principally directed to the promise of an eternal dynasty for David (7:5-7), he begins with an apparent rejection of David's idea of building a temple and he appeals to Israelite tradition that Yahweh dwelt only in a tent just as the Israelites themselves had done at the beginning of their own national existence (7:6).

The theological meaning seems clear enough: 'There lies the truth of God's Presence linked to his genuine reign in men's hearts. God does not dwell materially in a place, he dwells spiritually in his faithful people.'[15] However, at the Incarnation God's presence assumes definitive form. The episode of the cleansing of the Temple dramatizes Jesus' conviction that he alone is the one, true temple (Mt 21:12 f.; Mk 11:15-17; Lk 19-45 f.; Jn 2:14-17). As such he is greater than the Jewish Temple in Jerusalem (Mk 12:6). And eventually the meaning became clear to the early Church. Jesus is *the* Temple, and his Church, which is his Body, is the *new* Temple (1 Cor 3:9, 16 f.; 2 Cor 6:16; Eph 2:19-22). The temple-image no longer stands for mere presence, but for an actual indwelling of God in his people (1 Cor 3:16; Rom 8:9-11). Each one personally and all together in their oneness are the temple of God because they are, first of all, the Body of Christ. And the principle of this unity is the Holy Spirit. It is through the Spirit and only through this Spirit of the Risen Christ that the community 'grows into a holy temple in the Lord', in which the Gentile Christians too are 'built together into a dwelling place of God in the Spirit' (Eph 2:20 ff.).

Therefore, to suggest, as Vatican II does, that the Church is a holy temple, is to propose that God not only manifests his presence uniquely in his Body but that, through his Spirit, he actually dwells within the community of the faithful. Indeed, the community of Jesus' disciples only becomes the Church through the Spirit. Apart from the Spirit, the Church is but an association of Christian believers, a religious society or establishment.

The biblical image of the Church as a holy temple is closely related to that of People of God, Body of Christ, and sacrament. The Church must be, uniquely, the public sign of God's presence and indwelling in history. But the Church must also be open to the witness of the Old Testament which reminds us that God cannot be limited to this community or that community. He lives in tents. His shrine is mobile. The Church as the temple of God must convey this idea to others through the style and manner of her own existence. She is a community which recognizes that God comes to dwell among his people principally in their hearts, not in their institutions. For the Kingdom of God is not a matter of brick and mortar but of the love of God in Christ—in and through the Spirit. The Church is made of 'living stones' (1 Pet 2:5).

At first glance, the temple-image seems to portray the Church in its sturdy, Gothic grandeur—an immovable rock in a world of relative values and moral weakness. But the mandate of the Lord that the Church should be the temple of God actually calls the Church *out* of the 'Temple precincts' (the root meaning of *ekklesia*) and into a world which is the only arena for the building of the Kingdom. The Church has entered the day when she must, once again, take up her abode in the tents of the city. Her institutional structures are about to go into the melting pot. The Church of the future will be more flexible and more fluid. But she must always be the unique point of God's presence and indwelling in history—his holy temple.

The Church as Spouse of Christ

The mere enumeration of the various biblical images of the Church can unwittingly give rise to an odor of theological triumphalism. Systematic, methodical commentary on these descriptive notions can easily acquire the likeness of a litany of self-praise. And for those who remain unimpressed with biblical images, the litany is meaningless verbiage. The point is that these diverse images of the Church in the New Testament are meant for the instruction of the community as such, and not for those outside. And they are meant to be taken primarily as goals, rather than achievements.

The Church must *become* the sheepfold of the Good Shepherd; the Church must *become* God's holy temple; the Church must *become* the Spouse of Christ; and the Church must *become* the Body of Christ. For the Church lives in a state of tension between the 'already' of the resurrection and the 'not yet' of the Lord's Second Coming. She is, in one sense, 'already' the Body of Christ—and, in another real sense, 'not yet' his Body. Therefore, systematic reflection upon these various images is not meant to soothe and to comfort, to inflate and to exalt. Honest, searching meditation on the Church of the New Testament should be an unsettling affair. From this side of the parousia the Church shall never have reason to suspend her efforts to conform herself to those images and standards according to which the Lord has created and commissioned her.

Article 6 of the *Dogmatic Constitution on the Church* states:

[The Church] is described as the spotless *spouse* of the spotless Lamb (Apoc 19:7; 21:2, 9; 22:17), whom Christ 'loved and for whom he delivered himself up that he might sanctify her' (Eph 5:26), whom he unites to himself by an unbreakable covenant, and whom he unceasingly 'nourishes and cherishes' (Eph 5:29), and whom, once purified, he willed to be joined to himself and subject to him in love and fidelity. . . . While she is on pilgrimage here on earth (cf. 2 Cor 5:6), the Church regards herself as an exile from the Lord so that she seeks and savors those things that are above, where Christ is seated at the right hand of God, where the life of the Church is hidden with Christ in God until she appears in glory with her spouse (cf. Col 3:1–4).

The principal biblical foundation for the spouse-image is St Paul's letter to the Ephesians. It should be pointed out that St Paul is not primarily interested here in constructing a theology of the Church. Rather, he uses the fact of Christ's boundless love for his Church as the theological basis for a husband's love for his wife: 'Husbands, love your wives, as Christ loved the Church and gave himself up for her' (Eph 5:25). This is not an unimportant point. Paul is herein discussing the demands of the Gospel in the married state. His concern is not to reassure the Church with the doctrine that Christ loves and protects the Church, but to remind Christian husbands and wives that they should love one another as Christ loves his Church.

The love of Christ for his Church, as that of a husband for his wife, is more a call to responsibility than a gentle summons to secure repose. The spouse-image is only an analogy. Christ is equally concerned about the nonchurched majority of mankind. He is the bridegroom for all mankind, and all mankind is the object of his compassion, favor, and tender mercy. But the Church alone has the task of publicly proclaiming this reality, that Christ does, indeed, love all mankind with the solicitude and protective concern of a husband, that in Christ all men have been accepted and reconciled to the God and Father of us all. The Church's mission is to announce this 'good news' with some measure of credibility. Her preaching acquires a credible ring when the Christian community itself lives as the Spouse of Christ.

This occurs when the Church obviously draws her support from Christ alone, rather than from political or economic sources; when she opens herself to his influence 'that he might sanctify her'; when she is so patently 'subject to him in love and fidelity'; when, through her activities here in this world, she evidently 'regards herself as an exile from the Lord so that she seeks and savors those things that are above'

—which means, of course, when she gives genuine witness to the future character of the Kingdom of God by reason of her detachment, her poverty, her self-emptying posture even in the face of the temptation of political, economic, and social preferment.

The Church as the Body of Christ

Although the encyclical letter of Pope Pius XII, *Mystici Corporis* (1943), represented a decided advance over earlier notions of the Church, some theologians interpreted the document in too narrow and too rigid a manner. The 'Body of Christ' was seen not so much as one of the primary biblical images of the Church but as its one, determining image, and this interpreted in an organizational, juridical sense. Consequently, the first draft of the council's decree on the Church placed the body-image on a pedestal of its own and simply appended the other biblical images (temple, spouse, sheepfold, etc.) to the paragraph on the Mystical Body. As rich and as fruitful as the body-image happens to be, this could have produced a partial view of the Church. For the Church and Christ are not absolutely and completely identi-fied. In one sense, the visible Church is identified with Christ, and yet in another sense it is not.

'The image of the mystical body,' writes Canon Charles Moeller,[16] 'must not be allowed completely to overshadow the others, for although it emphasizes profoundly the identity of the Church and Christ, it does not of itself express the face-to-face encounter between the Church and Christ, the submission and obedience the Bride owes the Spouse, the purification she constantly receives from him. . . . Moreover, the theology of the Church as the Mystical Body has developed well beyond the encyclical *Mystici Corporis*.'

This kind of remark, even when it comes from an official of the Congregation for the Doctrine of the Faith and an architect of *Lumen Gentium* itself, is practically incomprehensible to one who leaves no room for theological development. How can the theology of *Mystici Corporis* be surpassed and changed? Isn't this simply a question of words and terminology? Theology is the expression of faith. Faith cannot change, and neither can theology. Mustn't we begin all of our documents with the words: 'Of course, the Church has always taught that . . . .'?

Faith is, indeed, that unchanging commitment which the Christian gives to the Lord, but theology is but a human attempt to formulate and to make sense of that faith experience. The Gospels themselves are among the earliest written theology we have. They represent the attempt of the first disciples to make sense of their experience of Christ, an experience of his resurrection and an experience grounded on the sending of the Spirit. The earliest definitions of the Church at the councils represent the written formulation of the Church's reflection on the Word of God in Sacred Scripture. The conciliar definitions are subject to growth, development, and modification because they can never adequately express what is, at root, beyond the possibility of adequate expression. And so the history of theology (the Church's systematic reflection upon her faith) proceeds. Because her formulations will never be adequate, her theological task will never be at an end. How then does the approach and the structure of *Lumen Gentium* bring Catholic theology forward?

The Constitution accords much space to the body-image, and this is as it should be. But the context is different. Even though the body-concept is superior to that of the temple, sheepfold, or spouse, for example, it is not to be regarded as a separate category entirely. It remains *one* of the biblical images of the Church. It must be qualified and modified by these other images as well, and the spouse-image in particular.

Whereas, *Mystici Corporis* begins with the analogy of the human body, *Lumen Gentium* begins directly with the New Testament. The Church is a mystery. It is the sacramental presence of the Lord in history. It is a 'new creation' called together by Christ through his Spirit.

The Body is essentially sacramental. The members of the Body are united to the Risen Christ principally and initially in baptism: 'For in one Spirit we were all baptized into one body' (1 Cor 12:13). To be baptized into the Church is to be baptized into the Resurrection Body of Christ. And the second great sign of unity is to be found in the breaking of the Eucharistic bread: 'Because the bread is one, we, though many, are one body, all of us who partake of the one bread' (1 Cor 10:17). In this way all of us are made members of his Body, 'but severally members of one another' (Rom 12:5). This sacramental basis of the solidarity of the Body of Christ was a steppingstone to everything that would be detailed in Chapter II on the People of God, Chapter III on the hierarchical structure of the Church, and Chapter VII on the heavenly Church.

The difference of perspective between *Mystici Corporis* and *Lumen Gentium* is particularly clear on the issues of Christ's headship and the problem of membership in the Body. *Mystici Corporis* insisted that Christ is Head of the Church because he is the most exalted of all creatures, and, secondly, because he rules and governs the Church as the 'royal citadel' of the Body. For Vatican II, Christ is Head of the Church because he is the principle and source of unity and 'he fills the whole body with the riches of his glory (cf. Eph 1:18–23)' (art. 7).

Because Christ is the Head of the Church, all members are to be modeled on him, 'until Christ be formed in them' (see Gal 4:19). The relationship, therefore, is one of intimate communion. The Church is a pilgrim community on earth, following the path he trod and, consequently, 'associated with his sufferings'. Christ the Head 'continually distributes in his body . . . gifts of ministries in which, by his own power, we serve each other unto salvation so that . . . we might through all things grow unto him who is our head (cf. Eph 4:11–16).' Finally, Christ is Head of the Church insofar as he 'shared with us his Spirit, who, being one and the same in the head and in the members, gives life to, unifies and moves the whole body . . .'.

And at the conclusion of the seventh article, the council document introduces the key relationship between Body and Spouse. The Church is, indeed, the Body of Christ. The community is identified with the Lord in a mysterious and mystical union. And yet, in another equally real sense, she is not identified with him. As Spouse of Christ, the Church is set apart from him, under his continual judgment. She cannot rest content that she *is* already his Body; she must become more fully his Body, for she is subject to him as his Spouse.

The question of membership raises another interesting point of divergence between *Mystici Corporis* and Vatican II. A perfect illustration of the need for an annotated, critical text of the council documents arises with reference to the key sentence in the eighth article: 'This [one] Church [of Christ], constituted and organized in the world as a society, *subsists in* the Catholic Church. . . .' (emphasis mine). A first, uncritical reading might suggest that the council is merely reaffirming the teaching of the encyclicals of Pope Pius XII, *Mystici Corporis* and *Humani Generis*; namely, that the Body of Christ and the Catholic Church are one and the same reality.

Conditions for membership in the Body of Christ are determined by the conditions for membership in the Catholic Church, and one of these conditions is communion with the college of bishops and the Pope. Under these terms, only

Catholics can be real members of the Body of Christ, because only Catholics are in such communion with the Apostolic College and the successors of St Peter. All others may be related to the Body of Christ by desire (*in voto*) to the extent that, if they actually knew that the Catholic Church was the one, true Church of Christ, they would spontaneously join it.

As a matter of fact, the phrase 'subsists in' was not in the original draft of the *Constitution on the Church*. Rather, it was selected as a more accurate and suitable replacement for the 'is' that appeared in the first draft. When the reader of *Lumen Gentium* is made aware of this development, he must realize that the council did not intend merely to reassert the teaching of Pope Pius XII. *Lumen Gentium* indicates a genuine development of doctrine from a strict and absolute identification of the Catholic Church and the Body of Christ toward a more dialectical and fluid relationship. The official reason offered for the change was that *de facto* there do exist outside the visible boundaries of the Catholic Church genuine elements of sanctification. This means, conversely, that the council acknowledged that we do not have all the elements of sanctification within the Catholic Church. The Body of Christ is larger than the Catholic Church, and not simply coextensive with it. We are a long way here from the Bellarmine–Tromp–*Mystici Corporis* axis.

The Holy and Sinful Church

We commonly make the distinction between the essential holiness of the Church, on the one hand, and the sinfulness of her individual members, on the other. Popes may be corrupt, bishops may be insensitive to the real needs of their people, chanceries may run roughshod over personal rights and human dignity, angry violence may erupt in so-called Christian neighborhoods on the race issue, politicians may betray their solemn public trust—but the Church as such remains untainted and untouched. With this kind of reasoning, it was always possible to hold at bay the perennial clamor for genuine Church reform. The real problem, one would insist against the critic, is not with the enduring structures and corporate life of the Church but with the unworthiness of some individual members. Moral reform (more prayer, penance, and sacrifice) is the proper response to any and every breakdown in the Church's missionary enterprise.

The Second Vatican Council did not close the door to personal moral reform. The *Decree on Ecumenism* warns that the whole movement for Christian unity is doomed to failure unless all Christians, of every community, return to the wellsprings of the Gospel and open their hearts to conversion and repentance. But the fundamental premise of this council has been that moral reform is not enough. There had to be a reform in ecclesiastical structures and corporate life as well. The Church itself must be renewed according to the dictates of the Gospel. The Church itself must follow the path of conversion and repentance. For, indeed, the Second Vatican Council did not accept uncritically the facile distinction between holy Church and sinful members: 'While Christ, holy, innocent and undefiled (Heb 7:26) knew no sin (2 Cor 5:21), but came to expiate only the sins of the people (cf. Heb 2:17), the Church, embracing sinners in her bosom, *at the same* time holy and always in need of being purified, continually follows the way of penance and renewal' (*Constitution on the Church*, art. 8, para. 3; emphasis mine).

This interpretation is confirmed (in somewhat ambiguous, if not contradictory, fashion) by Canon Charles Moeller: '*Sancta simul et semper purificanda* expresses admirably the paradox of a Church that is holy in its structure and constitution and yet must purify itself constantly because of the sinners present in its bosom. Here we touch upon the ecumenical problematic that was never solved by the oversimplified distinction between the Church (holy) and its members (sinners). In the Constitution the Church herself is said to be in need of constant purification.'[17]

The council is merely echoing here the themes of the Eucharistic Prayers for the First Sunday of Lent and the Fifteenth Sunday after Pentecost: 'O God, each year you purify the Church through the lenten observance. . . .' 'O Lord, let your abiding mercy purify and defend the Church.' The original distinction between holy Church and sinful members arises from a distorted ecclesiology. To separate the membership of the Church from the Church-in-essence is to assume a number of unsatisfactory theological principles: (1) that the Church is a salvific institution before it is a community of baptized people; (2) that the Church and the Kingdom of God are one and the same reality; and (3) that the Church is simply the Body of Christ, without taking into account the significance of the spouse-image which gives some theological balance to the body-concept.

The Second Vatican Council leaves little breathing space for the proponents of the old distinction. No longer can one legitimately explain away those deplorable instances where the Church in some particular parish, town, diocese, or nation may have become a countersign of the Kingdom. The old distinction will no longer work because it was never meant to work. There can be no genuine reform of the Church without genuine renewal in the Church. According to the perspective of Vatican II, this demands far more than rubrical changes in the Mass or allowing a few laymen to act on boards of trustees of some ecclesiastical institutions.

The Church as such is always in need of radical conversion to the Gospel. As this process of conversion occurs by the power of God's grace, reform must reflect and support this renewal. When this happens, the inevitable gap between holy Church and sinful Church will gradually close and the Risen Lord's presence in history will be the more unmistakably clear.

The Pilgrim Church

The first chapter of *Lumen Gentium* concludes with a summary and synthesis of the central themes of the entire opening section of the document: 'The Church, "like a pilgrim, presses forward amid the persecutions of the world and the consolations of God" [from St Augustine's *City of God*], announcing the cross and death of the Lord until he comes (cf. 1 Cor 11:26). By the power of the risen Lord it is given strength that it might, in patience and in love, overcome its sorrows and its challenges, both within itself and from without, and that it might reveal to the world, even though dimly, yet faithful, the mystery of its Lord until, finally, it will be manifested in full light.'

The Church is a community in history which is set between-the-times: between the death and resurrection of Jesus Christ and his Second Coming. Its principal task during this interim period is to confess its faith in the Risen Lord, to proclaim to the entire world that the meaning of human existence and of all history resides in the life and ministry of Jesus Christ, that everything that has happened, is happening, and will happen in history makes sense because he is risen from the dead and has been exalted by his Father.

The Church uniquely receives its strength and support from the Risen Lord. It is not simply a humanitarian social agency nor is it merely a group of like-minded people sharing a common social and historical perspective. Jesus Christ in his ongoing mission is so intimately related to this community that it can be called his very Body. And because the Church is the Body of Christ, she must reveal to the world the mystery of the Lord until he comes. The Church continues to reveal the mystery of the Father's love by continuing to reveal the mystery of the Risen Lord. It is the faith of the Christ that it is in the Church that we encounter the God of our salvation. Even in the face of sin and compromise with the Gospel, even when this community becomes on occasion a countersign of the Kingdom, the Christian firmly believes that we are confronted herein by the God of mercy, of forgiveness, and of love.

The Church, then, is the sacrament of Christ. Through her word, work, and ministry, all men should see the redemptive activity of the Lord himself. The Church continues his mission of suffering service. She empties herself to the dregs for the sake of all mankind that she might more effectively demonstrate the quality of love that God has poured forth in Christ. Nevertheless, the Church is not disappointed or frustrated in her mission if the majority of mankind does not rush to embrace her. She is not concerned so much with increasing her membership as she is in bringing men to accept and live the Gospel, if only implicitly. Her mission, like her founder's, is to heal, to unite, to bind together, to create a genuine human community where men are open to one another and bear one another's burdens.

When men live this way, they are already living according to the Gospel of Jesus Christ and are already within the Kingdom of God. And, indeed, this is the only absolute reality for the Church: not the Church itself, but God's Kingdom. All men are called to the Kingdom, and the

Church subordinates all her activity and concerns to this one end: that God's Kingdom may be realized more fully and that history may continue to move forward toward that day when God will be all in all, when his Kingdom will be brought to perfection.

Chapter 6

The Residue of Church-Centered Theology

The Second Vatican Council did, indeed, advance our under-standing of the Church beyond the uncritical notion that the Church is a visible, hierarchically structured organization which exists to save people by bringing as many men and women as possible within its orbit. The Church is a mystery, the sacrament of Christ, his very Body. The Church exists as a sign and instrument of God's Kingdom. Its mission is as much concerned with social justice and human progress as it is with the salvation of its individual members. But the council did not break completely with the Ptolemaic per-spective. The most obvious example of this is to be found in the thirteenth and fourteenth articles of *Lumen Gentium* and in the third article of the *Decree on Ecumenism*. It is also the underlying theme of the *Decree on the Missions*. The first two texts deserve to be quoted in full:

All men are called to be part of this catholic unity of the People of God, a unity which is a harbinger of the universal peace it promotes. And there belong to it or are related to it in various ways, the Catholic faithful as well as all who believe in Christ, and indeed the whole of mankind. For all men are called to salvation by the grace of God.

14. This sacred synod turns its attention first to the Catholic faithful. Basing itself upon sacred Scripture and tradition, it teaches that the Church, now sojourning on earth as an exile, is necessary for salvation. For Christ, made present to us in His Body, which is the Church, is the one Mediator and the unique Way of salvation. In explicit terms He Himself affirmed the necessity of faith and baptism (cf. Mk 16:16; Jn 3:5) and thereby affirmed also the necessity of the Church, for through baptism as through a door men enter the Church. Whosoever, therefore, knowing that the Catholic Church was made necessary by God through Jesus Christ, would refuse to enter her or to remain in her could not be saved.

And from the *Decree on Ecumenism*:

For it is through Christ's Catholic Church alone, which is the all-embracing means of salvation,[1] that the fullness of the means of salvation can be obtained.

Other conciliar texts could easily be interpreted in Ptolemaic terms by Bellarmine–Tromp ecclesiologists, although they are not so explicit as the items selected from *Lumen Gentium* and the *Decree on Ecumenism*. For example, the *Decree on the Missionary Activity of the Church* insists that the Church, which is the universal sacrament of salvation, must preach the word of God so that 'God's Kingdom can be everywhere proclaimed and established'. Moreover, 'the Church is summoned with special urgency to save and renew every creature'. The council's intention is 'that God's people, undertaking the narrow way of the Cross, may spread everywhere the Kingdom of Christ, the Lord and Overseer of the ages (cf. Sir 36:19), and may prepare the way for His coming'.[2] No doubt, some would continue to identify the Kingdom of God and of Christ with the Catholic Church.

In that case, the central theme and fundamental orientation of the *Decree on the Missions* becomes straight Ptolemaic ecclesiology. However, there is no reason to accept such an interpretation, because we have already seen (in the third chapter) that the identification of Church and Kingdom cannot be sustained, either biblically or theologically. Accordingly, I should prefer to concentrate on the texts cited above from *Lumen Gentium* and the *Decree on Ecumenism*, because these seem to endorse unequivocally the Ptolemaic point of view.

I shall structure my commentary around three questions: (1) Do the New Testament texts cited by the council (Mk 16:16; Jn 3:5) support the Ptolemaic thesis? (2) Can one agree that all men are, in fact, called to become the People of God without necessarily endorsing the Ptolemaic assumption regarding the Church? (3) Is the Church 'necessary for salvation' in exactly the same way as Christ is 'necessary for salvation'? All three questions are reducible to one: Is the council justified in its affirmation that the Church is, indeed, the *ordinary* means of salvation for all mankind?

The Argument from Sacred Scripture

Mark 16:16 reads 'He who believes and is baptized will be saved; but he who does not believe will be condemned' (see also Mt 28:18–20). What must be said, first of all, is that there is general agreement among biblical scholars that Mk 16:9–20 are not an original part of the Gospel. These verses are not found in the oldest manuscripts and were apparently not in the copies used by Matthew and Luke. This places the text in a more critical perspective, without necessarily discrediting its pertinence in the council document.

John 3:5 is another classic text which is always employed to support the Ptolemaic thesis: 'I tell you most solemnly, unless a man is born through water and the Spirit, he cannot enter the kingdom of God' (see also Rom 6:4). At first glance, it seems beyond question that the allusion here is to Christian baptism. And yet, Jesus is speaking with Nicodemus, who would not have understood anything about Christian baptism or the theology of rebirth associated with it. There is also some dispute about the insertion of the word 'water'. Bultmann insists that it can be attributed to the ecclesiastical redactor, who was attempting to introduce sacramentalism into the Johannine Gospel. Other scholars have suggested that the word is a later addition, although their reasons and arguments differ slightly. Protestant proponents of the later-addition theory include K. Lake, Wellhausen, and Löhse, and they have been joined in recent years by various Catholic Johannine scholars, including Braun, Léon-Dufour, Van den Bussche, Feuillet, and De la Potterie.[3]

But even apart from the obvious difficulties which textual criticism and exegesis poses for these texts, the passages have been misread and misinterpreted in a Ptolemaic vein because they have never been seen in the context of the biblical doctrine of *election*. G. Ernest Wright has suggested

If the primary and irreducible assumption of Biblical theology is that history is the revelation of God, then we must affirm that the first inference to be drawn from this view was not concerned solely with the power and attributes of God, but rather with the explanation of what God had done at the Exodus. That is, the initial and fundamental theological inference was the doctrine of the chosen people. . . . How else could Israel explain what had happened except by a conception of election? . . . Once such an inference was made, it was inevitable that those who collected and edited the earliest traditions of Israel should portray all history in this light. . . . The faith in a special election was one which always pointed forward to a future in which the full purpose of God would be manifest.[4]

What comes through clearly in the Old Testament is that God chose not the whole of mankind but a tiny remnant, Israel. This was the scandal of the doctrine of election, the scandal of particularity. Why should Israel, a nation of such obvious political immaturity and impotence, have been selected by God to be the vehicle of his designs in the long period of time before Christ? Why should God have spoken thus to Israel: 'Now therefore, if you will obey my voice and keep my covenant, you shall be my own possession among all peoples; for all the earth is mine, and you shall be to me a kingdom of priests and a holy nation' (Ex 19:4-5)? On the one hand, Yahweh's sovereignty knows no boundaries, for 'all the earth' is his. And yet from all the peoples of the world, he singles out one, not for a privilege, not for their own salvation, but for a special task. They are to be 'a kingdom of priests', a community separated from the world and consecrated for the service of all mankind (see also Gen 13:3, and the New Testament echo in 1 Pet 2:5, 9).

The doctrine of election is especially strong in the Deuteronomic tradition initiated in the eighth or seventh century. This later development conceives of Israel as having been set aside because of Yahweh's love for the forefathers of Israel and his oath to the fathers (Deut 7:6 f; 4:37 ff.), and not because of Israel's merits (Deut 9:4 ff.) or its numerical strength (Deut 7:7). Election places a responsibility on Israel which no other nation shares, and failure to meet this responsibility brings a more severe punishment upon Israel

(Amos 3:2). It cannot be emphasized enough that the counterpart of election was not reprobation, but simply nonelection for the purposes for which Israel itself had been chosen.[5] Certainly *Israel's* failure to fulfill its mission would bring reprobation upon its head, but since the other nations had not, in fact, been called, they would not be judged by this standard but by other, more universal standards.

This is not an excursion into scientific biblical studies. I want to be perfectly clear about my purposes at this point in Part III and in the book as a whole. The Church, which is the new Israel, has been made the object of a similar election by God. The Church will be judged by its fidelity to this call. But the great majority of men have not been called, and they will be judged by other standards, namely, by the standards of the Gospel itself.

So, too, election for a mission appears clearly in the servant of Yahweh in Deutero-Isaiah (Is 42:1; 49:7). The servant is chosen to have the spirit of Yahweh (Is 42:1), to establish justice in the earth (Is 42:4), to be a covenant of people and a light to the nations, to enlighten the blind and release prisoners (Is 42:6 f.; 49:6), and ultimately to bring deliverance by suffering (Is 53:1 ff.). As J. McKenzie and others have noted, it is more than coincidental that the application of election to Israel appears more frequently in Is 40–55 than elsewhere in the Old Testament. Israel, Christ, and the Church have been elected to fulfill a servant function. Each is a minority in the service of the majority. Each represents the whole. But the whole is not called to be the servant. The part is in the whole, but the whole is not meant to be in the part.

The Old Testament doctrine of election is carried over in the New Testament. St Paul reminds us that God has chosen the foolish, the weak, and ignoble things of this world (1 Cor 1:27 f.). Christians were chosen before the foundation of the world (and, therefore, before their merits could have been displayed) to be holy and blameless in the sight of God. Here in James 2:5 we have the rare idea of antecedent election combined with the responsibility of the elect. In general, the New Testament doctrine of election coincides with the theology of election in the Old. The Christian community has been marked out and set aside by the Father so that it might play some central role in the history of salvation. Once again, the counterpart of election is not reprobation, but simply nonelection. Some have been called, most have not. Those who have been called will be judged ultimately by their fidelity to the call and by their willing acceptance of the responsibilities which the call entails. Those who have not been called, and they are in the vast majority it would seem, will be judged by their response (implicit or explicit) to the demands of the Gospel itself. Those who respond to the Gospel in a positive fashion are living within the Kingdom of God. And the Kingdom is the only real touchstone of salvation. 'Many whom God has,' St Augustine wrote, 'the Church does not have; and many whom the Church has, God does not have.'

Let us return to the conciliar citation of Mk 16:16 and Jn 3:5. Even apart from the critical difficulties, these texts do not necessarily support the Ptolemaic thesis. These dicta make sense only in the larger context of the biblical doctrine of election. If, in fact, someone has been called to membership in the Church in order to participate in and execute the mission of the Church with respect to the Kingdom of God, then his failure to respond to this call will bring upon him the judgment of God. If the Christian-elect responds to the call, he will be able to work out his salvation within the remnant community of the Church. If he willfully ignores the call or shuns the responsibility, he 'will be condemned'.

Some may find this argument inconclusive. But what is the theological alternative? That Jesus meant precisely what he said? That only those who are baptized have a chance to be saved? This flies in the face of the entire Old Testament doctrine of election, diminishes the force of the belief that God wills all men to be saved, and displaces the Kingdom from the center of Jesus' preaching and ministry in favor of an unusual, almost narcissistic preoccupation with his own religious following. The *in re–in voto* distinction is a very weak attempt to resolve these pressing difficulties.[6]

What must remain absolutely clear is that God is the savior of all men (1 Tim 1:15; 2:4; 4:10) and that the ordinary means of salvation is through the living of the Gospel. One must lose his life in order to save it (Mt 16:25; Mk 8:35; Lk 9:24). Salvation is entrance into the Kingdom of God (Mt 19:25; Mk 10:26; Lk 13:23; 18:26). The salvation of man is God's final victory over evil. And God's final victory is achieved when his Kingdom is brought to perfection.

Consequently, the New Testament texts employed by the council (Mk 16:16; Jn 3:5) will simply not do. The Ptolemaic mind has distorted them, first of all by treating them uncritically, and secondly by reading them out of their proper theological context. In this case, that context is the central biblical doctrine of election and its dimensions of particularity.

Is the Call to the Church the Same as the Call to the People of God?

The council makes it very clear that all men are called to be 'part of this catholic unity of the People of God'. The second chapter of *Lumen Gentium* is concerned specifically with the question of the People of God, and the chapter ends on the same note: 'In this way the Church simultaneously prays and labors in order that the entire world may become the People of God, the Body of the Lord, and the Temple of the Holy Spirit, and that in Christ, the Head of all, there may be rendered to the Creator and Father of the Universe all honor and glory.'

Is the council merely reaffirming the Ptolemaic thesis here? It would seem so. All men, the council insists, are called to the People of God, and the People of God and the Church appear to be one and the same reality. One of the authors of the *Dogmatic Constitution on the Church*, Yves Congar, proposes that this is, indeed, the case: 'Should we call the People of God the sum total of all the individuals saved, even apart from positive and public revelation? The Council does not. It prefers the expression . . . of *ecclesia universalis*, which includes all the elect from Abel to the very last . . . . The People of God, in its existence and structures as a people, are those who know God and serve him in a holy way.'[7] Congar suggests that the People of God in its historical, concrete, and public form, is identified with the Church. Thus, if all men are called to be 'part of this catholic unity of the People of God', all men are called to membership in the Church as such. If they do not actually join the Church, they will be saved—if at all—by reason of some relation to the Church. The Church is, in this argument, the ordinary means of salvation for all.

But even present-day Catholic theology offers an alternative to Congar's traditionalism. Karl Rahner has concluded that all men are God's People already. They are joined together by an objective bond consisting in the fact that they are called to salvation, that they belong to a saved humanity whose existential situation is modified by this very fact:

. . . membership of the People of God is one of the determining factors of a concrete human nature, since every human being is necessarily and indissolubly a member of the one human race which really became the People of God by the divine Incarnation. Therefore, when someone totally accepts his concrete human nature by his decision of free will (the questions as to the conditions required for this need not detain us in this context), and thus turns his concrete nature into an expression of every one of his free decisions for God, his free action gains an expression which is at the same time also an expression of the proper, supernatural salvific Will of God. For this decision in freedom necessarily consents also to that membership of the People of God which, in continuance of God's Will of the Incarnation of his Word, constitutes an historically verifiable expression of the Will of God for the inner bestowal of grace on man as a person.[8]

Membership of the People of God, in turn, is ordered to membership of the Church in the proper sense. Accordingly, Rahner insists that his position does not impair the thesis that the Church in the proper sense is necessary for salvation. Those who are in the People of God but not in the Church are at least related to the Church by a *votum Ecclesiae*[9]. Congar cannot accept Rahner's opinion, but he admits that Vatican II neither accepted nor rejected it.[10] As a matter of fact, the difference between Rahner and Congar is insignificant. Rahner, despite his intricate speculative efforts, remains wedded to the Ptolemaic proposition. Even so, his reflections on the scope of the People of God are useful for our purposes here.

Chapter II, article 9 of *Lumen Gentium* reads: 'Its [the People of God's] law is the new commandment to love as Christ loved us (cf. Jn 13 : 34). Its goal is the Kingdom of God, which has been begun by God himself on earth, and which is to be further extended until it is brought to perfection by him until the end of time.' All men are called to the People of God because all men are called to the new commandment of love, all are called to the Kingdom of God which is the substance and goal of all history. Those who live by the Gospel, if only implicitly, are within the Kingdom. If they are within the Kingdom, they are within the People of God. The Church is the public, concrete, visible remnant of God's People which has a special task over and above the responsibility of simply living the Gospel. The Church has the mission of publicly confessing that Jesus of Nazareth is Lord, that the Kingdom has been inaugurated in him. It has the further task of struggling here and now for the realization of the Kingdom. And, finally, it must offer itself as a model of what the Kingdom is and will be like. This is a special mission which members of the Church have. It is a mission committed to them by the mystery of divine election. Not all men are the object of such election, and merit or numerical strength are not the ultimate criteria for such a choice. As in the Old Testament, the counterpart of election is not reprobation, but simply nonelection.

It is possible, therefore, to read the council's statement on the universal vocation of the People of God in two ways: the first simply reaffirms the Ptolemaic position, for the People of God and the Church are one and the same thing; the second interpretation would view the People of God as larger than the Church and coextensive with the boundaries of the Kingdom. All men *are* called to the Kingdom, because all men are called to live the Gospel. But the living of the Gospel is not necessarily allied to membership in the visible, structured Christian community. My own judgment is that the council did, in fact, intend the first position and thereby was reasserting the Ptolemaic thesis. The larger context of articles 13 and 14 of *Lumen Gentium* confirms this opinion, and, more specifically, the use of the two New Testament texts and the reaffirmation of the 'ordinary means of salvation' doctrine, to which we now turn our attention.

Is the Church 'Necessary for Salvation' in Exactly the Same Way as Christ Is 'Necessary for Salvation'?

Lumen Gentium argues that, because Christ is 'the one Mediator and the unique Way of salvation', the Church, which is his Body, holds the same place in the economy of redemption. Traditional theology calls this transference of attributes the *communicatio idiomatum*. But even traditional theology employed this tool with great reserve and with careful qualification. Not everything true of Christ is true of the Church in exactly the same sense. I have already shown in Chapter 5 that the identification of Christ with the Church (symbolized in the body-image) has to be balanced off with the dichotomy revealed both in the spouse-image and in the Church-Kingdom relationship. With regard to the former, the Church is already the Body of Christ, but in an equally valid sense it is *not yet* his Body. Christ and the Church are intimately united as one body, and yet they are distinct as bridegroom and spouse. The one is subordinate to the other. The one owes the other fidelity, obedience, and trust. And with regard to the latter (the Church-Kingdom relationship), we know that Jesus identified himself personally with the Kingdom. However, the Church is not to be identified simply with the Kingdom. Thus, the Church and Christ are in some important respects different realities. It does not follow that because Christ is the one Mediator and the unique way of salvation for all mankind, that the Church, too, is the **one mediator** and ordinary means of salvation. What is to be said, then, of the council's insistence that 'it is through Christ's Catholic Church alone, which is the all-embracing means of salvation, that the fullness of the means of salvation can be obtained?'

The Church as a 'Means of Salvation'

Salvation is human wholeness. 'It does not primarily signify an "objective" achievement,' Karl Rahner notes, 'but rather a "subjective", existential healing and fulfilment of life.'[11] For the individual, salvation means personal transformation by the Gospel. A person who loves according to the imperative of Christ is already saved; he is already within God's Kingdom as it presently grows and develops. A community which loves in the same fashion is a social expression of the Kingdom, a public sign of salvation. And when all mankind is within the Kingdom, salvation will have attained its fullness.

Jesus of Nazareth won us our salvation by force of his entire life: his preaching, his ministry, his death, and his resurrection. In him, the radical possibilities of genuine human existence have been revealed and released. Because he lived, all men can live. Other men may approximate the character and quality of his life, but none can improve upon it. And this is precisely the central conviction of Christian faith: 'Jesus is Lord.' Jesus is the one who uniquely and most dramatically reveals the meaning of life and all history. Everything makes sense in him and because of him.

And so there is only one reason for the Church's existence. If the Church cannot do this job, it has no reason to exist at all. If it cannot or will not work to bring men together, if it cannot devote itself full time to healing the fractures in the community of mankind, if it cannot uphold principles of justice and charity and peace, if it will not place itself at the disposal of others in the fulfillment of these goals, then it has no reason or justification for being.

The Church exists for the sake of the Kingdom of God. It exists to proclaim publicly that love is the principle of life and history. It exists to work and struggle and empty itself in the service of love. It exists as a kind of model of what the human community can and must become through love. God's Kingdom does, in fact, exist wherever his will is accepted and lived. And his will has never been more perfectly embodied than in the life and ministry, the death and resurrection, of Jesus of Nazareth. Jesus Christ and the Kingdom of God are one and the same reality, insofar as the reign of God is realized perfectly in him. Jesus is uniquely the 'man for others', utterly without selfish concern, the one through whom the reality of God (which is love) becomes transparent. It is in this sense that Jesus of Nazareth is *homoousios* (of one substance) with the Father, and it is in this sense that the Father was in Christ reconciling the world to himself (2 Cor 5:19).

All men are called to live in this manner, to realize to the fullest the potentialities of the human spirit. History cannot succeed otherwise. The alternative is hell, which is essentially life without love, life without community. And life without love or community is nonlife. Hell is essentially the extinction of life. The Christian works, therefore, with the conviction that history will succeed and that human existence makes sense because Jesus is the Lord of history and of life. Because of this conviction and this hope, the Christian must always be the revolutionary. He is never satisfied with things as they are. The work of building the Kingdom is an open-ended task. It is beyond our capacity and beyond our history, because it is ultimately a work of the Lord himself. And so there can be no moment in time when the Church can rest assured that we have achieved the Christian order. Until the end of history, the Church will be praying: 'Thy Kingdom come!' And the Church's actual struggle for the Kingdom will lend credence to the prayer.

Jesus, therefore, is the one Mediator and the unique way of salvation because reconciliation and salvation are the fruits of love alone, and Jesus is the personification of love, *homoousios* with the Father. The Church, on the other hand, can only approximate the perfection of Jesus, but, for good or for ill, she has been given the task of being both the public sign and the principal instrument of the Kingdom of God. This is not something which is intrinsically necessary. Its necessity for salvation (in the sense in which we have described it) derives from the will of God in Christ that there should be, in fact, some such public sign and instrument of his Kingdom in history. So the Church has become *a* necessary means of salvation by reason of divine choice. But this is a long way from saying that the Church is *the* necessary means of salvation, that men and women will be evaluated ultimately by the degree of their distance from the manifest Church and by the corresponding degree of their culpability for not affiliating with this Church in whole or even in part. This flies in the face of reality, as I have been arguing throughout this book. Insofar as Vatican II held fast, if only timidly and anxiously, to this particular theological conception of the Church, the council, too, set itself at odds with reality. Failing to make the break with Ptolemaic ecclesiology and failing to see through to the implications of the fuller ecclesiology which the council did propose, Vatican II was far less radical than it really ought to have been.

'The Council will be either the fulfilment of a great hope or else a great disappointment,' Hans Küng wrote on the eve of the first session. 'The fulfilment of a *small* hope would

—given the grave world situation and the needs of Christendom—be in fact a great disappointment.'[12] No great hopes can be fulfilled so long as the Church, Catholic or Protestant, Anglican or Orthodox, clings covetously to its Ptolemaic presumption. To the extent that Vatican II did so cling, to that extent was it a failure, and not merely 'a great disappointment'. However, there is some basis for optimism because the council did, indeed, advance considerably beyond the absolutism of the Bellarmine–Tromp position. It is truly remarkable that the council was able to accomplish as much as it did, given the problem of its theological schizophrenia. Had it completely dislodged itself from the Ptolemaic thesis, there would not have been so much agonizing and so much compromising when it came to writing its famous 'schema thirteen' (*The Pastoral Constitution on the Church in the Modern World*). Once the Copernican Revolution is accepted, so many other matters fall into their proper place. Some of the concrete, pastoral implications of this revolution (as well as its daughter Einsteinian Revolution) will be proposed in the next and final section, Part IV.

Part Four

TOWARD
A NEW THEOLOGY
OF THE CHURCH

Chapter 7

Who Should Belong to the Church?

A responsible reconstruction of ecclesiology should indicate its implications in sufficient detail to make clear the possibilities and limitations of its method. I should like to think that these final chapters will serve to dispel any residual ambiguity or confusion. In applying the Copernican and Einsteinian principles to concrete, pastoral issues, I hope to provide a deeper understanding of the principles themselves. The intention is that there be no exit or escape from the thesis of this book. One either accepts this concept of the Church with all its implications, or he rejects it outright as being out of harmony with the authentic tradition of Christian doctrine and theology. My hope is that I shall not overlook any major issue of Church life and work, or faith and order, that could significantly illuminate the main lines of the argument.

I shall raise, at the outset, the most fundamental question of all: Why be a Christian? Why affiliate with the Church? As a corollary to this question I shall ask: Why be a Catholic Christian? In this connection I shall discuss the case of Charles Davis and the larger problem of how the call to membership in the Church should be issued (the questions of apologetics, revelation, and religious freedom).

A second major area of inquiry will concentrate on the effective implementation of the Church's mission in the light of the Copernican and Einsteinian principles. Herein, I propose to discuss the ecumenical movement, liturgy, diocesan and parochial structures, 'Church power', and the inter-relationship between the magisterium, theology, heresy, and conscience.

It ought to be noted that I am not asking the question, 'Who *belongs* to the Church?' but rather 'Who *should* belong to the Church?' In terms of a pre-Copernican ecclesiology, the answer is clear: 'All men should belong to the Church, because Jesus Christ founded the Church to make available to them the means of salvation.' But I have already insisted that the pre-Copernican conception of the Church is theologically untenable, and so, too, is that answer. Membership in the Church is not a matter of advantage. The Church member does not have a running headstart over the rest of mankind. He is not necessarily more secure in his hold on salvation. Like Israel, the Church is God's 'chosen people' in the sense that it has a special job to do, not in the sense that it is a favored child, morally, intellectually, or spiritually. The counterpart of election is nonelection, not reprobation.

Why should one man be a Christian, a member of the Church, and another man not? Why should one man believe, and another withhold belief? Why should one man accept the universe as radically personal, and another interpret it by an image of impersonality: of chance, of functionalism, of the laws of physics, of the absurd? What evidence does either one have for the course he has charted? 'Among us thrives a brotherhood of inquiry and concern,' writes Michael Novak, 'even of those who disagree in interpreting the meaning of inquiry—the meaning of human spirit—in the darkness in which we live.'[1]

Despite the fabricated certitude of the older apologetics, absolute evidence simply does not exist. The nonbeliever could be right. Nevertheless, it is the Christian's conviction that his own posture of belief has its source outside of himself, that his faith is essentially a response, that there is a giftlike character to human existence. Our *'quest* for the sense of existence is met by the *gift* of a sense for existence. [Man] experiences this initiative from beyond himself in various ways. Insofar as it supports and strengthens his existence and helps to overcome its fragmentariness and impotence, he calls the gift that comes to him "grace". Insofar as it lays claim on him and exposes the distortions of his existence, it may be called "judgment". Insofar as it brings him a new understanding both of himself and of the wider being within which he has being (for the understanding of these is correlative), then it may be called "revelation"'.[2]

The invitation to explicit Christian faith and the call to membership in the Christian community are one and the same thing. Church membership is one of the major options in life. The one who makes this option does so with the conviction that it is a matter of responsibility rather than casual preference, that he becomes a Christian because that which is ultimate in reality has summoned him. The mystery of election is at the heart of the Christian understanding of life and history. There is no explaining it. One can only come to terms with it. Christian faith and the Church make no sense apart from the doctrine of election.

Accordingly, one does not become a Christian in order to live a better life. The possibility of human fulfillment is equally present outside the Church's borders.[3] Membership in the Church must always be the response to a giftlike invitation to share in the responsibility which the Church has to fulfill in history. Men are drawn to the Church because they are haunted by the figure of Jesus of Nazareth. In him resides the meaning of life and history. He is the Lord, and no other. And since Jesus was among us to proclaim the Kingdom of God, to realize it here and now, and to demonstrate its meaning by the quality and style of his own life, the Christian seeks to participate in this mission, to be a public sign and visible instrument of the Kingdom which he came to inaugurate and establish. The human person who is drawn to the Church is not interested in the cause of the *Church* but in the cause of the *Kingdom*. The Church is a means to an end. The Kingdom, and not the Church, is the reality which must attract.

Does this mean that the Church should relax her missionary efforts, or that she should shrink back with embarrassment at the approach of a non-Christian seeking admission into the community? Not at all. Membership in the Church is a sublime vocation. Men are elected by God to become affiliated with the Christian community so that they might share the task of giving explicit witness to what has happened, what is happening, and what will happen in history. The Christian is the one who must publicly attest to his faith in the Lordship of Christ, that all human life and history make sense because Jesus is Risen. And the Christian community has the unique responsibility of announcing this fact to the world, of committing itself to the task of bringing about the Kingdom of God here and now, and of showing others what it really means to live in Christ. Therefore, the Church must preach the Gospel with the real hope that some, who are in fact called by God to membership in the Church, will respond to the preaching and will see where their true vocation lies.

But the Church cannot be conceived as a kind of giant umbrella, under which a segment of mankind huddles to avoid the drenching of the sinful world. Membership in the Church confers a responsibility and a mission. Apparently, God calls relatively few men to assume these burdens, and these are not always the best of people. The Christian community itself is often the chief stumbling block to the Gospel. But God calls in spite of this weakness. Indeed, he works through this weakness, just as he worked through the weakness of Jesus. His Son was in our midst not as the Lord of the universe, but as the Suffering Servant of God (Phil 2:5–11). And that is how he continues to come through his Church.

The overwhelming majority of mankind, however, works out its relationship with God apart from the Christian community. God loves all these people with equal intensity, even those the Christian normally dismisses as his enemies: 'Although the Lord shall smite Egypt severely, he shall heal them; they shall turn to the Lord and he shall be won over. The Lord, our God, shall heal them' (Is 19:22). The love and mercy of God embrace the nonchurched as well as the churched, for all men are called to the Kingdom, all men are called to accept the Lord, at least implicitly: 'Truly, I say to you, as you did it to one of the least of these my brethren, you did it to me' (Mt 25:40; see the whole passage, vv. 31–46). This is the supreme test—the only test—of their acceptance or rejection of the Gospel, and the Church member is measured by it as well. Some are called, and some are not. The problem is not who belongs, but who *should* belong? 'For the last thing the Church exists to be is an organization for the religious. Its charter is to be the servant of the world.'[4]

Why Should One be a Catholic Rather than a Protestant, an Anglican, or an Orthodox?

Assuming that not all men are called to membership in the Christian community, is it also proper to assume that not all Christians are called to membership in the Roman Catholic communion? This may seem to be an entirely silly question to most non-Catholics, but it is not at all a frivolous issue. The ecumenical implications should be obvious enough. For if, indeed, all Christians are meant to be Roman Catholics, then the ecumenical movement—from the Catholic side—must be seen as a not-so-subtle attempt to bring the wandering sheep *back* to the one, true Church of Jesus Christ.

This question does not yield so easily to the Copernican and Einsteinian principles. After all, one can accept the Copernican thesis with reference to the Church as a whole, without necessarily surrendering his conviction that the Church of Christ should be one, and that the center of its unity should be the interrelated realities of the Eucharist, the college of bishops, and the Pope. The question of unity *within* the Body of Christ is an entirely different matter from the question of the place and function of the Church in the larger context of history.

First of all, what is it that distinguishes the Roman Catholic communion from other communities within the Church? The simplest possible response is to direct the reader to the third chapter of the Second Vatican Council's *Dogmatic Constitution on the Church (Lumen Gentium)*. Therein, in its starkest, most synthetic terms, is to be found the heart of distinctively Roman Catholic ecclesiology. Whereas the distinctive difference between the Christian and the non-Christian lies in the fact of baptism and the explicit confession of faith in the Lordship of Jesus Christ, the distinctive difference between Roman Catholicism and every other form of Christianity is its understanding of ecclesiastical office and, more specifically, the papacy.

The distinctively Roman Catholic understanding of the structure of the Church is outlined in the first paragraph (art. 18) of the third chapter. It begins with the observation that Christ instituted a variety of ministries in the Church for the nurturing and constant growth of the People of God, and that these ministers, who are endowed with sacred power, are servants of their brethren. Most non-Catholic communities could accept this without much difficulty. The council proceeds, however, to specify these ministries. Jesus established his Church by sending forth the apostles as he himself had been sent by the Father (Jn 20:21). 'He willed that their successors, namely the bishops, should be shepherds in his Church even to the consummation of the world.' With the affirmation of an episcopal structure, many lower-church Protestant denominations depart from the consensus. The final stage of disengagement is attained when the council insists: 'In order that the episcopate itself might be one and undivided, he placed blessed Peter over the other apostles, and instituted in him a permanent and visible source and foundation of unity and fellowship. And all this teaching about the institution, the perpetuity, the force and reason for the sacred primacy of the Roman Pontiff and of his infallible authority, this sacred synod again proposes to be firmly believed by all the faithful.' The remainder of the chapter merely develops the themes in these initial propositions.

The Catholic is one who, while recognizing the bond of unity he has with other Christians within the Body of Christ, is convinced that the heart and center of this Body resides in the Roman Catholic communion. The Catholic believes that the source of unity in the Church is the Eucharist and that the ministerial or hierarchical foundation of the Eucharist is the college of bishops with the Pope at the center and head. There are degrees of incorporation in the Church, and the norm of incorporation is one's proximity to these sacramental and collegial realities. The Catholic, therefore, would share the perspective of Bishop John Robinson when he wrote that 'it is impossible to be a biblical theologian without being a High-Churchman'.[5] There may, indeed, be areas for discussion, such as the precise meaning of infallibility, or the proper relationship between Pope and bishops, or the theological understanding of the presence of Christ in the

Eucharist, and so forth. But for the Catholic, a Church without a college of bishops, without the chief bishop as the successor of Peter, or without the Eucharist itself, is no Church at all. The Body of Christ is larger than the Roman Catholic communion (in fact, it is as large as the number of baptized who explicitly acknowledge the Lordship of Jesus), but there can be no Body without these Roman Catholic elements. And this brings us to the case of Charles Davis.

One should not be or become a Catholic unless he sees the value and significance of its distinctively sacramental and structural character. Charles Davis left the Roman Catholic community because he no longer believed in these structural realities. For him the traditional motives of credibility had lost their force. The Roman Catholic Church is not the visible embodiment of Christian faith, hope, and love, as the First Vatican Council insisted it must be, nor can its hierarchical claims be substantiated from Scripture and history.

What is to be said, first of all, about the theological ramifications of such a departure from the Roman Catholic community; and, secondly, what can be said of Charles Davis's line of argumentation?

It should be pointed out, at the beginning, that Davis broke with the Roman Catholic Church as it is presently structured (he even suggests that he would reconsider his relationship with it if that Church were to change essentially[6]) and not with the Christian faith as such. And since one cannot be a Christian apart from the Christian community (Davis agrees with this, too), he is still within the Body of Christ, even though he has shifted his place inside it.

Faith is not an ideological thing (although its objective, intellectual aspect cannot be denied). Faith is a commitment of the whole person; it is an orientation, a fundamental way of looking at life and history. Christian faith means that we accept Christ as the Lord of history and of our own lives, that life and history make no sense apart from him. And so one can sever his relationship with the Roman Catholic Church without necessarily surrendering one's faith. Undoubtedly, there is some change in the faith-commitment of one who leaves the Church, but this change is one of specification and not necessarily one of substance. If it were a question of substance (i.e., of the essence of faith), then we should have to conclude that the faith of non-Catholics is illusory. But not even conservative Catholic theology teaches this, and the documents of the Second Vatican Council (the *Decree on Ecumenism,* in particular) actually point in the opposite direction.

The Christian faith of a Catholic differs from that of a Presbyterian, for example, in specific aspects. The Presbyterian would not agree that the fullness of Christian faith cannot be realized apart from visible communion with the college of bishops and the Pope. This is an important difference, to be sure, but it does not strike at the very essence of the Christian faith; it is not something, in other words, that would distinguish a Christian from a non-Christian. In point of fact, the Catholic and the Presbyterian agree in the essentials of faith: both confess that Jesus is Lord; both share a common baptism; both share a common reverence for Sacred Scripture; for both, the source and root of the Christian life is in the spirit and idealism of the Gospel. In 1966 the Holy See allowed a Presbyterian woman to receive Holy Communion with her Catholic husband at their wedding Mass. She did this without renouncing her Presbyterian affiliation or becoming a Catholic.

Some Catholic theologians of another vintage would insist that movement within the Body of Christ is never justifiable unless the movement is directed toward the Roman Catholic center. Charles Davis, therefore, is not to be regarded as a member of Christ's Body. He is an apostate. A Catholic who rejects even one element of his Catholic faith implicitly rejects the whole of divine revelation. But this argument assumes that the Catholic continues to believe that the article in question is divinely revealed and that the Catholic Church has the authority to determine what is of divine revelation and what is not. However, this does not describe the Davis case at all. His recession from Catholicism is initiated precisely because he could no longer accept, as divinely revealed, certain specifically Catholic articles of faith. He does not reject divine revelation as such, not even implicitly. He simply questions whether or not this particular doctrine has, in fact, been revealed by God. Consequently, Davis (and anyone in a similar situation) must be accorded, at the very least, the same place as a non-Catholic Christian who is 'in good faith'. Traditionally, Catholic theology has referred to such a person as inculpably in heresy, i.e., in good faith. It is not legitimate to exclude theologically a Charles Davis from the Christian community. He has simply (and I do not use the word casually) altered his place within the Body of Christ.

The second question I posed above is much more difficult to answer: What is to be said of Charles Davis's arguments? Or, conversely, can anything positive be said for being and remaining a Roman Catholic?

Davis puts the challenge very clearly: 'If everyone openly declared what he did not believe, what were the limits of his acceptance of doctrines officially regarded as authoritative, we might see more clearly where the unity of Christian faith truly lay, whether it was in fact embodied and expressed in the present hierarchically structured Church. I can at least ask that those who question my departure should make clear the sources and limits of their own belief and disbelief. I should then know on what basis to discuss my position with them.'[7]

Since Davis overtly left the Roman Catholic Church because of his evaluation of the traditional motives of credibility, any positive justification for remaining within that community should not ignore these items. I must say, if only parenthetically, that I, for one, do not 'question' Charles Davis's departure from the Catholic Church; furthermore, I am not even sure that he has, in fact, departed at all. What does come through in his book is that Charles Davis is still a good deal more conservative than I am.

Davis insists, first of all, that the Roman Catholic Church as such is no longer a sign of faith, hope, and love, and he develops his argument in some detail.[8] When the First Vatican Council proposed that the Roman Catholic Church is and must be a credible sign of the Gospel, the prevailing ecclesiology in the Catholic Church was that the Roman Catholic community and the Body of Christ were simply coextensive. (This was to be reaffirmed and reinforced by *Mystici Corporis* and *Humani Generis*, as we have already seen.) Accordingly, it is not merely the Roman Catholic community but the whole body of Christian churches which are, or must be, collectively the sign of the Gospel of Jesus Christ. I do not wish to evade Davis's challenge to Roman Catholicism by side-stepping it with a semantic tour de force. However, I do suggest very bluntly that Davis's critique of the Church is not nearly radical enough, because it is not nearly broad enough. Certainly, the Roman Catholic Church is not alone in portraying an ambiguous (at the very most) sign of the Gospel. One need only reflect on the unholy alliance between many American Protestant churches and the politics of racial segregation and discrimination. South Africa poses yet another field for honest meditation. The point here is not to throw dust in the air or hide behind a 'plague-upon-both-your-houses' ruse. But unless Davis is prepared to argue that Roman Catholicism alone is a zone of untruth, etc., he must see that the signs of credibility are somewhat tarnished for the Christian Church as a whole. In which case, the question is not 'why be a Roman Catholic?' but 'why be a Christian?' For if, indeed, Jesus of Nazareth has an absolute claim on our consciences, should we not expect the company of his disciples to demonstrate, by the quality and character of its life, the validity and credibility of this claim? Davis, of course, admits that no single Christian church adequately embodies the signs of credibility and that is why he has, thus far, refused to join any one of them. But this seems to avoid the issue. One cannot be a Christian apart from the Christian community. And one is a member of the Christian community whether or not he attends services in a specific church or has his name on the membership lists of some denomination or local parish. Baptism and explicit faith in the Lordship of Jesus constitute such membership. If the Christian community as such does not offer a credible witness to the Lordship of Jesus, then its baptismal and sacramental rituals are a farce and one should creatively disaffiliate with the entire reality.

Beyond this, Davis's demands for the signs of credibility seem too absolute in themselves. Although various Catholic theologians are reluctant to admit this (and perhaps Charles Davis's own conservative orientation would make him similarly reluctant), the Church itself is sinful.[9] Thus, we cannot fully expect the sign of holiness to stand erect in solitary splendor. A sinful Church is more than likely to convey a sinful image at some time or another. The signs of credibility will always be ambiguous. They are usually such as neither to command assent nor render their rejection inevitable. Charles Davis has read these signs one way (and I do not see how anyone can question what he sees), but men of equal integrity and theological competence have continued to read them in another, balancing off the debits against the assets and finding the latter in sufficient display so as to foreclose any peremptory departure.

Davis draws the same conclusion from his analysis of Scripture and history.[10] He looks again to the New Testament and finds nothing there to support the Roman Catholic claims. On the other hand, the German exegete Heinrich Schlier found himself compelled to move in the opposite direction, and precisely on the basis of his New Testament studies. Again, the point is not to confuse the issue by introducing a foreign element into the discussion. But what Schlier's decision illustrates is that New Testament investigations can open a two-way street. Once more, the signs of credibility are ambiguous. One cannot absolutely reject either position: the Roman Catholic or, in its various manifestations from High-Church to Low-Church ecclesiology, the non–Roman Catholic. The evidence from the Bible and from history is neither so clear as to compel assent, nor so weak as to undercut entirely the distinctively Catholic commitment. And where does all this leave us?

With Bishop Robinson, I reaffirm that it seems impossible to be a biblical theologian without also becoming a High-churchman. The Church of the New Testament is hierarchically and sacramentally structured. 'Early Catholicism,' as Ernst Käsemann and Hermann Diem would now admit, comes closer to the primitive situation than Harnack, or Luther, or most others in the Reformation tradition have wished to concede.[11] But this is not to say that the Catholic concept of the Church is necessarily realized in the concrete, canonical structures of the present Roman Catholic Church. On the contrary, there is a great disparity between the *theology* of 'Catholicism' and its *canonical* expression. And the principal reason for this disparity lies in the unbiblical and untheological notion of *jurisdiction*. Canonically, jurisdiction refers to the public power of ruling the Church, and the

Code of Canon Law insists that such power is of divine institution (can. 196). In the practical order of things, jurisdiction of the so-called 'lower clergy' makes sense only in the context of papal and episcopal power. And yet in the New Testament there is no basis for the kind of jurisdiction which either the Pope or the bishops currently exercise. The monarchical episcopate simply did not exist, nor did the papacy as an office possessing full and supreme, ordinary and immediate jurisdiction not only over each and every church but even over each and every pastor and lay person in the Church (see can. 218, nos. 1 and 2).[12]

In the New Testament there is no real theological difference between a bishop and a priest. The bishops (*episcopoi*) and the elders (*presbyteroi*) are one and the same (Acts 20:28; Titus 1:5), and together they form one college (Acts 20:17; Titus 1:5). The only clear difference in the realm of sacramental orders is between bishops and elders, on the one hand, and the deacons, on the other (Phil 1:1). It is the deacon, and not the priest, who is the assistant of the bishop and especially at the Eucharistic table. The idea of canonical jurisdiction is an entirely postbiblical construction. It is not necessarily opposed to the biblical understanding of the ministerial priesthood, but neither is it something which one must defend and accept if one is to remain faithful to the Catholic expression of the Christian faith. Theologically, the Roman Catholic must accept Peter and the college of bishops—and, indeed, the whole idea of the ministerial priesthood. Canonically, he must also accept Peter with jurisdiction and the episcopacy with jurisdiction. But what is canonically imposed is of a far different order from what is theologically imposed. To reject the canonical creature is not necessarily to reject the theological reality.

For example, it is one of the great theological and pastoral tragedies of our time that the average Christian's attitude toward the papacy and papal authority should be formed almost exclusively within the context of the birth-control issue.[13] Those on the left, who seem to have drifted off into cynicism, and those on the right, who seem to have intensified their militancy, ironically share a common 'tradition' regarding the papacy. Both extremes have accepted—the one implicitly, the other explicitly—the post-Vatican I ecclesiology which exalted the Pope to a kind of supertheologian. Both want the Pope to speak definitively and without ambiguity on every controversial issue and to rule one position or the other out of theological order.

This attitude is reminiscent of a favorite ecclesiastical game in the 1940's and 1950's when Catholics would quote encyclicals at one another. But in the light of the theology of Vatican II and beyond, what is being fashioned today is a more critical attitude toward the papacy (and, indeed, toward the whole concept of papal-episcopal power): a critical attitude which eschews both cynicism and militancy, and an attitude which accepts the papacy for what it must be —the leading moral authority in the Church which, nevertheless, shares our human condition in all things, including sin and error. This change of attitude is dramatically reflected in a sermon of Episcopal Bishop C. Kilmer Myers of the Diocese of California (June 4, 1967). Bishop Myers urged Anglicans and Protestants to acclaim the Pope as 'the chief pastor of the Christian family, and . . . the holy father in God of the Universal Church. We need someone to say, as chief pastor in Christ, that the world-wide community of Christians must exert its massive power to halt war and conflict in the world. We need a chief pastor who will lead us in the fight against poverty and the powerlessness of peoples on the earth.'

Perhaps the bishop was thinking of the charismatic pontificate of John XXIII, or even of Pope Paul VI's prophetic call for the end of all war in his United Nations' address (October, 1965), or his innumerable interventions in the cause of peace in southeast Asia, or his recent encyclical letter *Populorum Progressio*, wherein he challenged mankind in its selfishness and condemned all forms of political, economic, and cultural exploitation. For it is precisely in proclaiming the Gospel that the Pope fulfills his role as chief pastor and holy father. It is not his responsibility (nor within his area of competence) to teach a particular economic philosophy or a specific biological or medical interpretation of some human problem. He proposes the Gospel context within which these enterprises are to be carried out, and he does not hesitate to raise his voice when God's Kingdom is subverted. Indeed, it is Peter's relationship to the Kingdom that is central. The office of chief shepherd is not to be defined primarily in terms of Church structures, but in terms of the Church's mission to proclaim and realize the reign of God in the world. The ministry of Peter is for the sake of a unified and effective mission and not for the sake of organizational uniformity.

But why should the Catholic respond with some measure of enthusiasm to the call of the Pope on issues of war and peace or social justice when this same Catholic may seem cool, if not openly hostile, on other issues, such as the question of birth control? Is there an inconsistency here? Have we reverted to the 'pick-and-choose' polemics of the forties and fifties? Inconsistency becomes a problem if one's starting point is the uncritical ecclesiology of the early twentieth century: the Pope is the only theologian that matters in the Church and papal encyclicals (or official statements of any kind) are our pipeline to absolute truth.

But it has become impossible today for many of these Catholics to support this kind of theology of the papacy. The papacy has spoken authoritatively on contraception, they would insist, but it is 'naïve' about the Vietnam war. There is to be no compromise with the clear strictures of Pope Pius XI's *Casti Connubii*, but we can imagine all sorts of 'factors' to ease, mitigate, and effectively destroy the force of the Pope's resounding argumentation in *Populorum Progressio*. I must leave the far right wing to resolve its own inner contradictions. My appeal here is to those who have grown cynical about the papacy but who still recognize the call of the Gospel in so many papal utterances and gestures. There is no problem of inconsistency here if the attitude toward the papacy is critical in the first place, and if this criticism is radically sympathetic (which is the only kind that can bear fruit in the long run).

On the birth-control issue, the Pope's present disposition does not seem to reflect an overriding consensus in the Church: neither among theologians nor, more importantly, among sensitive and serious Christian married couples (and this is a source which no theologian can ignore). The social teachings, on the other hand, reflect the consensus of the Church insofar as it has been expressed at the Second Vatican Council: 'Christ was sent by the Father "to bring good news to the poor, to heal the contrite of heart" (Lk 4:18), "to seek and to save what was lost" (Lk 19:10). Similarly, the Church encompasses with love all those afflicted by human infirmity and recognizes in those who are poor and who suffer, the image of its poor and suffering founder. It does all it can to relieve their need and in them it strives to serve Christ.'[14]

Thus, the real and only foundation of the Pope's authority is the Gospel itself. He is subject to it, just as the entire Church is subject to it. When he proclaims the Gospel as chief pastor and holy father of the Christian family, his voice finds an echo throughout the Christian community. If the proclamation is genuinely evangelical, the Holy Spirit will see to the echo; if it is not, he will see to the static. And what has been said in reference to the Pope applies equally to the college of bishops and to the individual bishops of specific dioceses. Authority in the Church is for the sake of service. Its foundation is not canonical jurisdiction, but the Gospel itself. To the extent that the individual Pope or bishop is a sign of the Gospel, to that extent is his teaching authoritative. The function of the Pope or the bishop is to be a sign of the unity of the Body of Christ. The bishop is the symbol of unity and the spokesman for the Body in a given area where there is a true assembly of smaller local communities. The Pope is the sign of unity and the spokesman for the international fraternity of local churches. The Catholic position is that such authority and such symbols of unity are, in fact, required by the New Testament concept of the Church.[15]

What is to be said, then, about the prerogative of papal infallibility? This seems to carry the concept of the papacy far beyond the purely evangelical authority described above. What should be noted, first of all, is that the First Vatican Council did not really define its understanding of papal infallibility. It insisted only that the Pope possesses the same infallibility 'with which the divine Redeemer willed his Church to be endowed'.[16] The council also severely limited the exercise of this infallibility: the Pope must be speaking as the shepherd of the entire Christian community, as the head and center of the college of bishops, and he must be addressing himself to matters of the Gospel itself. The Catholic belief is that when the Pope acts in this capacity, consciously identifying himself with the entire college of bishops and the whole Church (including all the non-Roman Catholic Christian churches!), he speaks as the international spokesman of the Body of Christ and is its symbol of unity. Insofar as his words reflect the actual faith of the whole Church, they must correspond essentially with the ultimate meaning of the Gospel itself. That is, if the Holy Spirit is indeed with the Church, the Church as a body cannot be led into radical and permanent error with regard to its fundamental understanding of the Word of God.

The more conventional Catholic understanding of papal infallibility makes of it a meaningless and useless enterprise. The proof of this lies in the rarity of such papal utterances. Since Vatican I the Pope has but once employed the tool of personal infallibility, and that was to define the bodily assumption of the Virgin Mary into heaven. Not only was this an unwise gesture (the ecumenical implications were clear enough), but it was theologically unjustifiable. The Church cannot propose one philosophy or another for absolute belief. But behind the doctrine of the Assumption lies a specific philosophy of nature, an understanding of man as composed of two separate elements (body and soul) which, upon physical death, separate leaving the body behind and allowing the soul, now in its Platonic release, to go directly to God for judgment. It was in this philosophical context that the papal declaration considered the last state of the Virgin Mary. Unlike the rest of men, she was never separated from her mortal body. Body and soul, she was 'assumed' into heaven. (We leave aside the cosmological implications of this particular doctrine.)

Charles Davis is completely right when he insists that 'an infallible intervention by the Pope is conceivable only when there is no longer any need for its authority, because the problem belongs to the past and the results of the debate are secure . . . . That is why what may be called a practical infallibility has to be assigned to ordinary papal teaching in order to make papal authority actually operative.'[17] The conclusion must be, therefore, that infallibility applies only to the Church as a community, and to the Pope as spokesman of the community and symbol of its unity (under the conditions which I have described above). Personal papal infallibility, as understood by post–Vatican I theologians, and admittedly by Pope Pius XII himself, is a theological fiction and cannot be supported or sustained.

To undercut personal papal infallibility is, a fortiori, to undercut what Davis calls 'practical infallibility', i.e., the infallibility which is illegitimately extended to papal utterances which do not, in fact, meet the rigid conditions of Vatican I. The birth-control issue is a good case in point. The college of bishops, in an extraordinary abdication of responsibility, has allowed the Pope to reserve the final decision to himself. But the decision cannot be exclusively his. He must take into account the convictions of the entire Church (including the non-Romans!) as well as the convictions of all the bishops who represent various sectors of the Church (including the non-Roman!). Furthermore, the supposition that the Pope, or any ecclesiastical authority, can speak definitively on the purely biological and medical aspects of the question is also out of order theologically. An authoritative statement, symbolizing the consensus of the entire Christian community, cannot do more than delineate the Gospel context within which the medical and biological judgments can be made and the issues resolved. Consequently, no papal statement, produced in isolation from these elements, can lay claim to the religious adherence of any member of the Church. Even if the issue has been resolved one way or the other by the time this book appears, the principles which are implicit in this controversy remain valid.[18]

Where does all this leave us with regard to Charles Davis? If Davis does, in fact, insist 'that an hierarchically structured Church has ceased to be an appropriate vehicle for Christian mission',[19] and if he means this in an absolute sense, then he and the Roman Catholic remain substantially apart. If, however, he can accept the general implications of Bishop Robinson's position that it is impossible to be a biblical theologian without at the same time being a High-churchman (i.e., having some notion of an hierarchically structured Church, in the New Testament sense and not in the canonical, jurisdictional sense), then his and the Roman Catholic positions are more nearly alike.

Finally, unlike Charles Davis, I do not regard the event of Pope John XXIII's pontificate as a kind of historical fluke. Pope John demonstrated that there is a place and a necessary function within the Church for a chief shepherd who can enunciate through word and example what the Gospel is all about and what mission the Christian community has to fulfill. Pope John is one of the many good reasons for remaining within the Roman Catholic communion, and Charles Davis has capably enumerated some of the many reasons for leaving or remaining apart from the Roman Catholic Church. Neither side has an absolute claim in terms of the evidence adduced. Neither side need be embarrassed or unsettled by the decision taken or reaffirmed. And neither side can dare to overlook the common challenge facing both of them: to refashion the entire Christian Church into the unmistakable sign of Christ's presence in history. In this regard, *neither* side has any ultimate achievements upon which to rest.

The Call to Church Membership: How Should It Be Issued?

The classic means of evangelical communication is through the preached Word: 'For "every one who calls upon the name of the Lord will be saved". But how are men to call upon him in whom they have not believed? And how are they to believe in him of whom they have never heard?

And how are they to hear without a preacher?' (Rom 10:13-14). We are considering the question in the context of the general thesis of this book. Not all men are called to the Church, but some, indeed, are called. The hope of the Church is that all those who have, in fact, been elected by God for membership in the Christian community will be able to respond to this invitation. And the normal manner in which this invitation to membership is to be issued is through the proclamation of the Word. This leads us to a discussion of some of the related theological concepts: revelation, apologetics, and religious liberty.

Revelation

Before the theological renewal of the last few decades, revelation was often described, even by professional theologians, as 'the communication of those truths which are necessary and profitable for salvation', while faith was defined as 'the intellectual assent given to those truths'. No serious theologian today would regard these definitions as adequate to the realities in question. Faith is not an exclusively intellectual act, and the verbal aspect of revelation is only a part of the total mystery of God's self-disclosure. The fact that theologians—and, as we shall see, the Second Vatican Council—have advanced beyond the more limited perspective of early twentieth-century theology is no guarantee that the Church at large has been following along at a respectably close distance. On the contrary, this may be one further instance of the gap that exists between the theology of Vatican II and the theological understanding of many members of the Church.

The popular misconception of revelation which assumes that its content consists of statements and propositions (e.g., 'There are three persons in one God') could not have arisen unless there were some justification for it. Revelation must be expressed in language, otherwise it would remain a purely private affair. There would be no possibility of communicating and sharing the revelation with others. And this, in turn, would rule out the existence of the Church itself, for the Christian community comes into being in response to the revealed Word.

Consequently, theology cannot argue for the elimination of creeds and other specific formulations of faith. Such a proposal would be an overreaction to the intellectualist misconception of revelation and faith. It is true, of course, that Christianity is a way of life, but it will soon lose its identity if its ethic becomes separated from its doctrine. Even so, the emphasis on statements and propositions in the older theology of revelation was an unfortunate one. It really identified the statements of faith with the revelation itself. But this is not the case at all. The formulations follow, and are not identical with, the act of God's self-disclosure and our own free response to him.

This should not be too difficult to accept, for it is simply in accord with the manner in which we come to know and understand anything. We must first of all have an experience of the reality. The experience comes before the concept. Once we have experienced the reality, we seek to clarify its meaning in our mind. We 'formulate' our concept to provide a basis of comparison with our other experiences or with the experiences of other people. For example, a man witnesses a serious automobile accident. Later, he stands before a judge in court and attempts to recapture in words the tragedy of that experience. The judge then transposes his testimony into legal terminology in order to render it legally intelligible.

A similar situation occurs in the mystery of revelation. Man has an experience of God and then he attempts to express this experience in concrete language so that he may share it with others. The experience itself is the revelation, while the subsequent verbal description is the means of conveying the revelation-experience to others. And what is most important is this: because the source of the experience is God, the revelation-event cannot be expressed adequately within the limits of human language. And not only is the language inadequate; it may even be distorting. That is why it must be subjected to careful scrutiny by the Church.

The *Constitution on Divine Revelation* of Vatican II describes revelation, not as a series of statements or propositions, but as the mystery of God's self-disclosure (see Chapter I of the document). The council indicates that God reveals himself through the realities of creation, through the historical events of the Old Testament, and uniquely in Christ. Neither the written word of the Bible nor the official teachings of the Church are revelation. They are mankind's reflection on the revelation-experience which they have had through nature, history, and Christ.

This does not mean, however, that revelation is now a thing of the past, something to be interpreted, handed on, and preserved intact. Christ still lives. He continues to reveal the merciful and loving Father each time a man responds to the needs of another. The presence of God is manifested in those who live according to the Gospel of Christ (and this must include even the non-Christian, who constitutes the majority of mankind). For whoever lives in such a way that his relationships with others are marked by generosity, sensitivity, sympathy, and genuine concern, is living according to the Gospel. And one who encounters such a person is in the presence of a revelation-event, for the presence of God is manifested in the gracious neighbor. Yet one man 'sees' and another does not, because revelation is not a natural phenomenon, subject to mathematical verification.

'In the lives of those who, sharing in our humanity, are

however more perfectly transformed into the image of Christ, God vividly manifests his presence and his face to men. He speaks to us in them, and gives us a sign of his kingdom.'[20] The Kingdom of God is realized wherever the Lordship of Christ is acknowledged. And the Lordship of Christ is acknowledged, at least implicitly, wherever his Gospel is lived, when men love one another and bear one another's burdens. The Church cannot divorce her ministry of proclamation from her call to live the Gospel, corporately. Even as she proclaims the Gospel, the Church must show mankind what it means to live in Christ, what it means to be a gracious neighbor.

Revelation can be described more precisely as a personal union in knowledge between God and a human person in the context of an historical community. It should be pointed out, however, that revelation is not an exclusively Christian thing, nor is the historical community to be identified necessarily with the Church. God does not communicate with Christians alone. There is no law of logic or of theology to prevent him from drawing near and disclosing himself to those outside the Body of Christ. On the contrary, revelation occurs wherever and whenever man has an experience of the presence of God. It is an event which happens not outside of man but in his human consciousness. The fullest experience of God takes place in the consciousness of Jesus of Nazareth, so that to know him and to share in his understanding is to know the Father.

Given the infinite depths of their experience of Christ and of his Spirit, and given the severe limitations of human language, the apostles could not have hoped to recapture fully this experience in their preaching and in their writing. The Church realizes this when she reflects on the fragmentary testimony of the apostles. She tries to recapture not only *their* experience but also *her own* contemporary experience of

Christ. And, finally, the individual Christian tests *his own* experience by the standard of the Church's corporate, historically realized experience of Christ. In this sense there is no revelation unless God is now acting and unless a human consciousness is now responding. As such, revelation is immediate and occurs in the present experience of the community.

But it must be reaffirmed that the immediacy of revelation in the human consciousness does not rule out the scrutiny of the Church. Thus, to use an extreme example, if a Christian believed, with the conviction of a revelation-experience, that the 'ideals' of the American Nazi Party are to be accepted and applied, he could not enlist the support of Christ for his prejudices nor could he attribute his conviction to a revelation-experience. Racism thoroughly contradicts the total experience of the Church and flies in the face of the clear teachings of the Gospel, which is the privileged written expression of the apostles' and the early Church's experience of Christ and of his Spirit. In other words, the teaching of the Second Vatican Council that revelation continues into our own day and comes to us through the presence of God in individual persons does not necessarily open the door to arbitrary revelation-experiences. Each 'experience' must be tested by the Church, and measured against her own corporate experience as well as the privileged experience of the apostolic Church.

The whole point of the current reexamination of the theology of revelation is to emphasize that revelation is a present, here-and-now reality in our lives; that it is not something to be relegated to the past, as something that happened then and there and which is no longer operative in our own time. God continues to speak to us, and the unique point of contact is Christ: yesterday, today, and for ever. He continues to address us even today. He confronts us

in the proclamation of Sacred Scripture, in the sacraments
(the Eucharist, in particular), in the guidance of the teaching
Church, and in persons who embody his love for mankind.
By each of these means, Christ may yet draw us to himself.
Note the word, 'may'. The mere proclamation of Scripture
is not always a revelation-event, nor is the liturgy, or the
teaching of the Church, or the gesture of the gracious
neighbor. There can be no revelation unless the movement
of God takes hold in the human consciousness. Some men
'see' and others do not (or will not).

Finally, does the notion of a continuing, here-and-now
revelation mean that the deposit of revelation actually in-
creases? Not at all. God has said all that he wished to say or
could say in Christ. There is no going beyond the Word.
This is the age of the continuing Pentecost, of the movement
of the Spirit to conform the minds of the faithful to the mind
of Christ where revelation occurs in its fullness. Is this so
difficult to accept? What we are doing here is merely
applying to revelation what traditional theology has always
proposed regarding the Eucharist, for example. What Christ
accomplished through his life, death, and resurrection was
perfectly sufficient for our salvation. Traditional theology
refers to these events as 'objective redemption'. Yet we
believe that the 'objective redemption' must be made present
somehow if it is to have any meaning for those of us who are
far removed from the events of Good Friday and Easter. The
application of 'objective redemption' is called, in traditional
theology, 'subjective redemption'. Some Protestants (not all,
certainly) have insisted that the Catholic derogates from the
perfection of the 'objective redemption' when he places such
stress on the Mass and the sacraments. It is ironic, indeed,
that much of Catholic theology in the early twentieth
century adopted this same 'Protestant' attitude with regard
to the mystery of revelation. Contemporary theology and

the Second Vatican Council are proving to be a useful corrective, not only with regard to the problem of revelation to the non-Christian but also for the whole problem of 'religionless Christianity'. What is revelation for one for whom the Bible, the liturgy, and the teachings of the Christian Church have no meaning?

God speaks here and now to them and to the Christian in and through the neighbor who cares, who lives as 'a man for others'. The gracious neighbor gives us an insight into the nature of reality itself. To put it in a way that is both theological and philosophical: the gracious neighbor demonstrates that Being itself is gracious. Some men, in the presence of the gracious neighbor, will be drawn by the Spirit of God, to become a member of the Body of Christ and to give explicit witness to the fact that God has so loved the world that he gave his only begotten Son. Still others may respond differently, i.e., in the manner in which the majority of mankind responds. They may catch something of the contagious spirit of the gracious neighbor and live in like manner in their relationships with others. These, too, have accepted the Gospel of Christ, if only implicitly. But, after all, it is not the man who says, 'Lord, Lord!' who will enter the Kingdom of God, but only he who actually does the will of our Father in heaven. And what is his will? That we should love one another as God himself has loved us in Christ.

St Paul himself adopted this fundamental principle when he declared: 'Be imitators of me as I am of Christ' (1 Cor 11:1). More meaningful even than Paul for our time is Pope John XXIII. He provides us with a kind of test case for this new theology of revelation. God revealed himself through John's spirit of warmth and love, his openness to all peoples, of every race, nation, and religious belief and nonbelief; through his concern for the humble and the neglected, for the 'castoffs' of society; through his spirit of resignation and nobility in the face of suffering and death; through his concern for justice, so forcefully expressed in his encyclical *Mater et Magistra*; through his concern for world peace, for harmony and friendship among all peoples, as expressed in *Pacem in Terris*; through his concern for Church unity and Christian renewal. It is as if God were calling us to these tasks through the word and ministry of John.

Why is it that the life and ministry of Pope John XXIII struck such a responsive chord in the hearts of all mankind, believer and nonbeliever alike? Why is it that people, so long bored and unimpressed with grandiose pronouncements, suddenly took an interest in *Pacem in Terris*? Why is it that people, so long indifferent and inattentive to the large-scale and well-organized charitable enterprises of the Church, suddenly were touched by the example of the Good Shepherd visiting the sick, the orphans, and those in prison? Why is it that people so long cynical and bitter about the problem of evil found inspiration in the sickness and suffering and dying of John XXIII?

In and through this giant of a man and this luminous sign of the Gospel, there shone forth a power and a beauty and a strength not often experienced on such a world-wide scale. Pope John was so transparently 'a man for others', a gracious neighbor, a suffering servant of God—without pretension, without self-seeking, without arrogant concern for dignity and rank. Working in and through the humble Pope was the one about whom St Paul wrote: 'Though he was in the form of God, [he] did not count equality with God a thing to be grasped, but emptied himself, taking the form of a servant, being born in the likeness of men. And being found in human form he humbled himself and became obedient unto death, even death on a cross' (Phil 2:6–8).

The contemporary theology of revelation is eminently

pastoral and practical. The Christian must be ever more sensitive to the presence of God in the people and in the reality around him. But what is more important: the Christian must so open himself to the Gospel of Christ and so live it without compromise that the presence of God—the gracious God in the gracious neighbor—will intrude itself, breaking into our lives and our history.[21]

Apologetics

At the base of the council's *Decree on Ecumenism* and its related *Declaration on Religious Liberty* is the assumption that the vast majority of non-Catholic Christians and non-Christians are sincere in their own religious convictions. This is obviously the more charitable thing to say about them, but is it really accurate? After all, isn't the Catholic faith capable of logical and rational explanation to the unprejudiced, open-minded inquirer? Can't we prove *that* God has revealed himself to mankind, *what* he has revealed, *through whom* he has revealed, and *wherein* that same revelation continues to be proclaimed and interpreted today? And if this is so, how can we assume that those outside the Catholic Church (and especially those outside the Christian community entirely) can be in good faith? Are they not responsible for failing to examine the evidence, or, having examined it, for refusing to accept the clear implications of the evidence?

The view that the *fact* of revelation can be established by natural reason appeared very late in the history of theology, occupied the scene for a few decades, and has since disappeared from the realm of serious theology. But during its period of ascendancy (particularly in the early part of this century), this opinion was very influential in the area of apologetics. It was disarmingly simple: once you have proved *that* God has revealed, then you can go on to believe the content of revelation with every confidence in the reasonableness of the act. It may be surprising to some that the theologians of the medieval period insisted that the fact of revelation is an object of faith, and is not perceived through natural reason alone. In the very same act by which we assent to God's revelation, we acknowledge that it is true and that it is of divine origin. In other words, we do not first establish by reason that it is of divine origin and only then accept it as being true.

Does this mean that there is no rational support at all for the Christian commitment? The First Vatican Council properly rejected not only Rationalism but also Fideism, for the act of Christian faith is not an arbitrary religious experience. What, then, is the situation? It is precisely this: Christian faith is *reasonable*, but not *rational*. And where is the difference? Faith is *reasonable* to the extent that it is not absurd to believe in the Lordship of Jesus and, indeed, it makes good sense to affirm that he is the ultimate norm of all life and of all history. It can be shown that one does not renounce all regard for the intellect when he accepts Christ and that life in Christ can be more meaningful than life without him. Faith is not *rational*, however, because it cannot be proved through reason alone, to the extent that an unprejudiced observer, under the impact of argumentation, would have no other choice than to believe—or violate his own integrity. The view that the fact of revelation can be known by reason alone is tantamount to making the assent of faith a natural act. The position cannot be sustained theologically. It has been condemned by the Church ever since the problem first arose in the Second Council of Orange in the year 529.

If the fact of revelation were attainable by natural reason, then God would no longer be the motive of Christian faith. Faith would be reduced to natural knowledge in which the Christian's assent rests ultimately on his own reasoning powers. Even though the Christian is believing 'supernatural' truths, the reason for his accepting them is the evidence encountered and endorsed by his own reason. And if the arguments to support the fact and the truth of revelation were beyond dispute, then we could no longer maintain the freedom of the act of faith. It would simply be a question of bowing before the evidence. But if, on the other hand, the force of the arguments is limited, then the assent which rests upon them must be limited also, and faith thereby loses its absolute character.

Therefore, the teaching of the Second Vatican Council in its *Decree on Ecumenism* and its *Declaration on Religious Liberty* is built upon sound theology. The council did not accept the view that the fact of revelation can be known by reason alone. Consequently, Vatican II rejected the assumption that non-Catholics (and all non-Christians) are, by and large, in bad faith or simply too dull or too preoccupied to see and accept the evidence.

Traditional apologetics adopted still another, broader approach which recent biblical studies have effectively undermined. The argument went something like this: the Catholic Church is a divinely established institution because Jesus Christ is its founder. And Jesus is a divine person because he claimed to be God and actually proved his claim through miracles and prophecies. We find the evidence for all of this in the New Testament. The New Testament is an historical document and its trustworthiness and authenticity can be established through historical and scientific means. Therefore, Christ is the Son of God and the Church shares in his divine authority. To hear the Church is to hear Christ.

However, measured by nineteenth-century standards of writing history, the four Gospels would be ruled out of court. The documents are not easily traceable to eyewitnesses, and the authors make no pretense to impartiality.

They write as believers. The diversities between St John and the Synoptics make it clear that the Evangelists themselves did not aim at photographic accuracy. On the contrary, the Gospels are religious testimonies addressed to us by the primitive Church. The portrait of Jesus therein is one structured by faith. The Evangelists are writing to testify to the faith of the primitive community and to transmit this faith to others. The question arises: Is the portrait credible?

First, despite the differences in approach and content, the picture of Jesus which emerges from the four Gospels is remarkably unified. Secondly, the New Testament faith about Jesus is proclaimed with the strongest conviction, as if the message had been communicated and manifested to them with blinding clarity. Thirdly, the New Testament doctrine about Christ is utterly novel. Nothing in the Jewish tradition would have predisposed them to accept the doctrine of the Incarnation and the idea of Jesus as the Suffering Servant of God sharply contradicted Judaism's hope for a political messiah. Fourthly, the apostles themselves were completely transformed into new men by the tidings which they bore. And, finally, the Christian message itself is not the type which is easily fabricated. Two thousand years ago it sparked a religious revolution, and even today its influence continues in every race and culture. The unique qualities of the Gospel message and the community that developed from it are such that the rational inquirer is hard-pressed to offer a satisfactory explanation.

The old 'historicist' apologetics fails because even the words and works of Jesus do not prove the truth of the Christian message in such a way that a coldly scientific investigator would feel obliged to assent. Even if the so-called historical method could transport us to the very foot of the Cross, it would still require an act of faith to attach any ultimate significance to the crucifixion itself. Secondly, the Gospels themselves fall short of what a scientific historian would consider optimum material for the events in question. The new apologetics, on the other hand, treats the Gospels as religious testimony, as expressions of faith. And this brings it abreast of the modern notion of history. Contemporary historians such as R. G. Collingwood reject the 'scissors and paste' approach to history,[22] so prevalent in the nineteenth century and in the older apologetics, which tried to combat nineteenth-century historicism on its own grounds.

In the final analysis there can be only one fundamental sign of credibility and that is Christian holiness itself, as realized individually and corporately. The Gospel can only ring true when men see the faith and hope of the Church sustained by a life and ministry of charity. As Cardinal Leger remarked on the occasion of his announcement that he would resign as archbishop of Montreal to work among the lepers in Africa, 'The glass of water freely given is still today the most convincing proof for the existence of God, who is present in the fevered face of a poor man.'

It was much easier in the old apologetical framework. A few arguments settled the matter. The new apologetics is actually more demanding. There can be no defense of the faith if there is no living of it. And the living of the Gospel is its strongest defense.[23]

Religious Liberty

I do not wish to minimize the extraordinary contribution of the late John Courtney Murray, S.J., but I must suggest that, once the Copernican Revolution in ecclesiology is accepted, the debate about religious freedom and toleration will be seen to have only historical interest. The arguments and counterarguments regarding the obligation of the state to recognize the true religion or to permit the public exercise of so-called false religions were based on the assumption that all men are, in fact, called to membership in the 'one, true Church of Christ'. Despite the obvious merits of the council's *Declaration on Religious Liberty*, the document continues to assume that all men *are* called to membership in the Roman Catholic Church: 'Therefore, it [this declaration] leaves untouched traditional Catholic doctrine on the moral duty of men and societies toward the true religion and toward the one Church of Christ' (art. 1, para. 5). The defect is a radical one.

If, however, all men are *not* called to the Church, the theological problem of religious freedom recedes abruptly and without ceremony. The state must, in fact, be neutral toward religious convictions except where, in its practical, political judgment, these convictions overflow into specific patterns of behavior and activity which obstruct the state's effort to implement the principles of social justice and public order. Lest there be any possibility of misinterpretation: the state could *never* justify the establishment of the Roman Catholic Church as the official religious organization of the nation itself, nor should the state give *any* religious community a position of favor and privilege within its social structure.

Christian faith is the product of divine election. That the political and civil rights of the non-Christian (or non-Catholic) should be infringed upon in any way is theologically absurd and morally indefensible. By the same token, religious groups have every claim on the protection of the law when it comes to the exercise of their own legitimate functions. Neutrality does not mean the exaltation of a militant antireligious secularism. In the final analysis, the issue of religious liberty is not a peculiarly Christian problem. It is part of the larger problem of political justice and equity for all. In that sense, Father Murray was correct to argue the case for religious liberty on the basis of *constitutional* principles and only secondarily on the basis of theological principles.

Chapter 8

The Mission of the Church

The Ecumenical Movement

The ecumenical movement represents a potentially grave threat to the Church and to the Gospel. The principal danger is not false irenicism or a kind of religious indifferentism. The risk is that the quest for Christian unity will make the Church even more excessively *church*-conscious and even less *mission*-conscious. The fact of disunity in the Christian Church violates the will of Christ that all his disciples might be one, and it also impairs the effectiveness of the common witness which the Church must give by means of its *koinonia* in the Spirit. The Church must offer itself as a model of the Kingdom. And since the Kingdom is to be identified with the human community as it gradually comes into being even now, between-the-times, the Church must be able to present itself as a kind of ideal community in which the highest values of the human spirit (truth, love, justice, hope, fellowship) are not only enshrined rhetorically but implemented without compromise or dilution. To the extent that the disunity in the Body of Christ weakens the impact of the Church's witness to the quality and character of God's Kingdom, to that extent must every Christian feel the sharp edge of the divisions.

One of the areas where this 'sharp edge' of division is most keenly experienced is in the issue of mixed marriages. In the past there was a tendency to look upon the partners of a mixed marriage as disloyal to their church. Today there is an increasing awareness among the churches that it is not the couple's love but the churches' dividedness which is disloyal, i.e., disloyal to the will of Christ. 'Mixed marriages,' notes the Ecumenical Commission of the Episcopal Diocese of Massachusetts, 'are not an evil to be mitigated, but an honest and natural relationship between human beings to be blessed and ministered to. In fact, such marriages contain the possibility of becoming a prophetic sign of the triumph of the love of the Lord over the division of the churches.'

But the ultimate goal cannot be the unity of the Church as such: a common understanding of Scripture and tradition, a common formulation and conceptualization of doctrine, a common liturgical practice, a common hierarchical and ministerial structure or polity. These can never be completely achieved to everyone's satisfaction. The Roman Catholic experience should demonstrate the illusory, futile aspect of such a goal. For despite an externally common doctrinal understanding, liturgy, sacramental life, and ecclesiastical organization, there is as much division of opinion and variety of 'spiritualities' in Roman Catholicism as there is in many other sectors of the Christian community. Complete theological, liturgical, and structural unity can never be achieved, and perhaps it should be said that such unity is not even a desirable goal. There can be no single theology, no uniform pattern of worship, no ossified form of church polity. The ecumenical movement must accept not only the Copernican Revolution (and thereby not look upon the struggle for unity as an attempt to make the Church more effective in dispensing salvation to an unredeemed world) but also, and especially, the Einsteinian Revolution. The Church is entering a period when her theology, her liturgy, and her structures are going into the melting pot. This is not simply a question of changing the husk or the shell, a kind of sleight-of-hand magic act. Something entirely new will come out of the cauldron, and the only similarity it must bear with the primitive Church of the New Testament is that it must be a community which explicitly acknowledges that Jesus of Nazareth is the meaning of all life and history and which dedicates itself, without qualification, to the task of building and sustaining the human community. It will be a community that reaffirms its link with the Jesus of history and the original company of his disciples by celebrating a Eucharist (however radically altered it may be) and it will be a community which takes upon itself the prophetic task of measuring the values and operations of society by the ideals and standards of the Gospel of Jesus Christ. Accordingly, this community will never be satisfied that it has achieved the Christian order of things because it will always proceed on the conviction that the perfection of the human community can only come as a grace, that the Lord himself must bring history to its successful conclusion, because love, which is the stuff of the Kingdom of God, is always a gift, i.e., something to which one responds but which no one can create as such by his own power and initiative.

There is a sense, then, in which we might say that we are called in these days to a 'secular ecumenism' as opposed to a 'churchly ecumenism'. And, of course, secularity should be understood in the terms of Part I of this book. Unity is worth struggling for because the Church has a fundamental responsibility to be the sign and instrument of God's Kingdom. A radically disunited Church can only provide an ambiguous witness as it awkwardly attempts to proclaim, to realize, and to signify the reality of this Kingdom. The witness is especially compromised and muddied by the contemporary issue of racial justice. This has been described as the 'acid test' of Christianity. If the Christian community cannot offer a common, stouthearted, unflinching witness on this issue, then the community itself has to reexamine the point of its very existence. Is it completely impractical and naïvely optimistic, however, to hope that the Church will ever be able to offer such a common witness on an issue such as this? It is an impossible dream if one remains committed to the pre-Copernican doctrine of the Church. If, in point of fact, one continues to insist that there is some advantage to belonging to the Church because it is the ordinary means of salvation for men, then we shall never overcome the menacing obstacle of moral stagnation and we shall never be out of earshot of the mournful moan of the Church's 'uncertain trumpet'.

The many who remain in the Church even though they have not, in fact, been called to the community, would surely reassess their relationship to the Church once the impact of the Copernican Revolution had been felt. There is no advantage to being a member of the Church in terms of ultimate salvation. If the 'Christian' cannot accept the Gospel in its explicit, verbalized form as proclaimed by the community itself, then this is a certain sign that the election has never been made in the first place or, if it has been made, the vocation was a temporary one and the time for departure is now.

The Church, in other words, is entering a time when she must not only lose members but she must have the courage and the faith to promote actively their disaffiliation. The process will never be complete within our history. The wheat and the chaff will continue to grow together. But the Church is not thereby exempt from the struggle. The ecumenical movement, therefore, is not primarily a question of reconciling this church and that church, or this theology and that theology. It is rather a matter of purifying and unifying the witness of the Church in the proclamation of the Gospel, in the struggle for the Kingdom, and in the erection of an unmistakable sign or model city of the human community. And this can occur without uniformity in theology, doctrine, liturgy, and structures. Again, the proof as well as the pattern is the Roman Catholic Church itself, which even now is the home of the widest possible theological, liturgical, and, to a lesser extent, structural diversity. And it is because of this that one should properly advise the ecumenist to look to Rome as the pattern for the future. As time goes on, it will become ever increasingly a useful standard for change, reform, renewal, and a good dosage of revolution. The Roman Catholic Church holds a unique place in the Body of Christ by reason of its numerical strength, its structural cohesiveness, and its theological and liturgical traditions. When this Church goes into the melting pot, the explosion will be far more powerful than any of us might have imagined. The surviving fragments will be the building blocks of the Church of the future, of the Church of the Einsteinian Revolution.

Intercommunion

In this larger theological context, questions such as intercommunion assume a dwarflike character. Even the Second Vatican Council suggests that Christian unity must proceed through common worship, as well as cooperation in matters of social concern. Ordinarily we are precluded from common worship because our worship is and must be a sign of unity. But because this unity does not always exist (except in an imperfect fashion), we have gone our separate ways liturgically. We have raised the question: 'Dare we eat the Lord's Supper together?' But there is another factor to consider as well. The Eucharist is not only a sign of unity but it is also the primary means of attaining the grace of unity. Even St Thomas Aquinas insisted that the principal effect of the Eucharist is the unity of the Church. And so the Christian community must also be prepared to ask a second question with equal seriousness: 'Dare we continue to eat apart?'

The *Decree on Ecumenism* states: 'Common worship . . . may not be regarded as a means to be used indiscriminately for the restoration of unity among Christians. Such worship depends chiefly on two principles: it should signify the unity of the Church; it should provide a sharing in the means of grace. The fact that it should signify unity generally rules out common worship. Yet the gaining of a needed grace sometimes commends it' (art. 8). The statement is characteristically guarded and carefully qualified; nevertheless, the council does concede the case in principle. The Church cannot simply dwell upon the notion that the Eucharist must be a sign of unity. Intercommunion is to be taken seriously because it is also a means of unifying the divided Body of Christ. The Christians themselves must decide whether or not sufficient unity exists and sufficient hope for deeper unity is present before proceeding with their common celebration of the Eucharist. This is a decision which only the local community itself can reach. The bishops, who are the overseers and the focal points of unity, must accord the greatest possible freedom in this regard lest by precipitous administrative action they crush what the Spirit himself has planted and watered, and to which he has given the increase.

Liturgy

Liturgy refers to the public worship of the Church, and the idea of Christian cult introduces us into a world of symbols, rites, and ceremonial expressions of faith. The very notion of worship has to be rethought thoroughly. First of all, worship is not for God's sake. He doesn't need such displays of human affection or respect. Worship is for man. Through worship, man acknowledges what he is and what he must become. Liturgy plays a role in helping man come to a fuller understanding of himself. And the immediate insight which worship provides is that no man, by himself, is the master of his own destiny. Man is nothing apart from the human community, and the human community, historically viewed, is nothing apart from the ultimate meaning which accounts for its existence and for its final achievements.

Christian worship makes no sense apart from Christian mission. Christians worship because it is an aspect of their responsibility for the Kingdom of God. Through the liturgy, the community is reminded of its election by God. Through the liturgy, the Word of God is burned more deeply into its heart so that there can be no mistaking its demands or its judgments. Through the liturgy, the Christian Church professes publicly that it has accepted the mission and it reaffirms its resolution to carry out this task. Through the liturgy, finally, the Church tries to demonstrate the quality and character of the Kingdom of God by its own life of *koinonia* in the Spirit.

But if, however, the Church is not engaged in its mission, there is neither reason nor justification for its celebration of the Eucharist. Without a real commitment to the Kingdom, the Church's liturgy becomes a ritual charade. The pre-Copernican notion of the Church makes much of the Eucharist but for the wrong reason. Faithful attendance at Mass becomes the primary means of visible solidarity; failure is mortally sinful. Just as the Church was regarded as important for its own sake, so was the Eucharist. But once the Church is plucked from the center of salvation history, the Eucharist and, indeed, the whole liturgy of the Church assumes a new dimension. The Eucharist, like the Church, is a means to an end, a means to realize God's Kingdom. Not all are called to the Eucharist; only those who have deliberately accepted the mission should celebrate it at all. More sins may be committed by reason of attendance at the Eucharist than by reason of separation from it. For those who eat and drink of the body and blood of the Lord, when they have not really accepted the Christian mission, eat and drink to their own judgment.

Therefore, we must be careful about a too-hasty endorsement of the council's statement that the liturgy is the summit and the source of the entire Christian life. This is true if one sees the liturgy as the sacramental side of the Christian mission. It is far from true, and it may even be positively distorting, if it is supposed to mean that the most important thing that Christians do is celebrate the Eucharist and the other sacraments. This is pre-Copernican theology in liberal-liturgical dress. For the only essentially important enterprise in which the Christian can ever be engaged is the task of creating here and now a community founded on the spirit of the Gospel of Jesus Christ. To the extent that liturgy helps this mission, liturgy should be employed and encouraged. However, undue concentration on matters of liturgical practice and reform must not be allowed to distract the Church from this overriding mission. And that is why, in the end, excessive episcopal control over the liturgy can have very serious theological and missionary consequences. Suppression and harassment in this area beget resistance and intrigue of every sort. The 'suppressed' and the 'harassed' finish by adopting the fundamental theological assumptions of the suppressors: that the liturgy and the Eucharist are ends in themselves. On the contrary, the Church has no business bringing gifts to the altar unless and until it is actively engaged in the work of reconciling brothers. The building of churches for the sake of worship must always be nearer to the bottom of the Church's theological and pastoral priorities. What is always a means can never be allowed to supplant the end.

The other sacraments must also be viewed in this same light. Baptism, I have insisted earlier, is not primarily a means of making one 'a child of God and an heir of heaven'. It is a public sign of divine election. It confers, for the first time, a sanctifying *mission*, not primarily a sanctifying *grace*. Infant baptism makes sense, if at all, because it demonstrates, as adult baptism cannot, that the initiative in the election is totally God's. He chooses even *ante praevisa merita*, before we have a chance to prove ourselves, and he never fails to confound us by his choice.[1] Confirmation takes the place of adult baptism when it is conferred upon one who was baptized as a child. Through confirmation, the Christian has the opportunity to ratify the election and to publicly commit himself to its faithful execution. Penance is not for the forgiving of sins. Like baptism, confirmation, and the Eucharist (and, indeed, all the sacraments), it is for the sake of the mission of the Church and that, in turn, for the sake of the Kingdom of God. When a Christian sins gravely (and this happens when, in some way, he violates the reality of the human brotherhood), he thereby impairs the effectiveness of the Church's witness to the holiness of Christ and his Gospel. Through this sacrament, the Christian who has thus sinned against the Christian community is restored and reconciled to the Church. Marriage inaugurates a new segment of the general human community. Through sacramental marriage the Christian publicly reaffirms his baptismal mission and directs it toward this new area of his life, for if he cannot realize God's Kingdom in this limited area of the world, he cannot hope to realize it historically or cosmically.

Holy Order, too, is for the sake of the community, but this time for the Christian community as such. The Church as the Church has specific needs. If it is to be faithful to its mission, it must be confronted again and again and again with the Word of God. The ordained minister accomplishes this through preaching. The Church must also realize that its mission is communal, that the realization of the Kingdom must be a corporate endeavor. And so the ordained minister presides at Christian worship where the awareness of the communal responsibility must emerge clearly and sharply. Holy Order, then, is for the sake of the Body of Christ, that it might live according to its inner nature and that it might become more fully what it already is. Finally, Anointing of the Sick is for the sake of restoring the infirm Christian to a life of effective service. It is a sacrament of the seriously sick, not of the dead or near-dead.

In the pre-Copernican framework, the sacraments are primarily means of salvation. Christ came to save people and the sacraments are his way of continuing his work even after he decided to return to heaven. And yet even fewer people 'receive the sacraments' than are members of the Christian Church. If these are, in fact, part of the ordinary economy of salvation, then most people—including a good representation of Christians of every denomination—are beyond the reach of Christ's saving work. However, once the sacraments of the Church are viewed in relationship to the nature and mission of the Church as such, and the nature and mission of the Church are viewed in the light of the Copernican and Einsteinian revolutions, then the awkwardness of the facts dissolves. And so, too, do most of the pages of the theological and canonical textbooks which, in the manner of cookbooks, speculate and legislate about the proper or improper administration or reception of the various sacraments. Let one example suffice for all: there is a common opinion that, in case of imminent death, a non-Catholic, nay even an atheist, could baptize the infant of Catholic parents, so long as he recites the right words, does the right things, and intends to do 'what the Church herself intends'. This concession is proposed because of the belief that human beings who die without baptism and before reaching sufficient maturity to posit one good act are probably consigned to Limbo, i.e., they shall forever remain apart from the immediate presence of God although 'naturally happy'. But the practice is theologically indefensible when baptism is seen in its proper context. It is the Church which mediates the call of God through sacramental baptism. That someone other than a representative of the community should baptize is as absurd as a member of the Knights of Columbus officially receiving a new member into the Masons. Only the missionary community itself can communicate the mission to someone else. Baptism is the public sign of the conferral of the mission. It is not the means of saving dying infants from the eternal isolation of Limbo.

Diocesan and Parish Structures

Father Robert Adolfs and others have argued recently that the Church is allied too closely with the idea of the residential community. When the Church celebrates the Eucharist, it becomes 'event'.[2] And it becomes 'event', given the present structures, in some neighborhood or other. This strong tie with the residential system has produced an individualistic, pietistic morality which relates only to the private sphere of one's life. It has little or nothing to say about the Christian's life in the public sector, where his attitudes and activities really matter: in the managerial hierarchy, the labor union, the community organization, the political party, and the various bureaucratic units that organize our lives. Consequently, many Christians retreat to moral questions about marriage and family life, as if this constituted the Church's greatest ethical problem of this century. Christian love is fulfilled if husband and wife 'get along'; matters of race, rat control, and riots are left to the political (i.e., 'nonreligious') order.

The Church itself is accorded special economic privileges because it performs one key function, without which society itself might fall victim to a collective anxiety neurosis. The Church allays our fears and uncertainties about death, by assuring us that what we do in this life does have ultimate meaning because there will be a reward (or punishment) hereafter. But by allowing itself to be pushed into the purely private sphere of life, the Church compromises its essential role of prophecy. By the commission of Christ, it must exercise a prophetic judgment over society at all times. It cannot draw back from the task of condemning selfishness and combating all forms of political, economic, and cultural exploitation. At times this must bring the Church eyeball-to-eyeball with the powers that be. No vested interest, no special privilege can compromise it in these moments of confrontation.

What is demanded in our time, therefore, is a radical restructuring of the Church according to the theology of the Church as the Servant of God and as the sign and instrument of the Kingdom. The Copernican Revolution reveals that the Church is not to be preoccupied with dispensing the means of salvation to neighborhood communities, and the Einsteinian Revolution will demand that the neighborhood community is not to be sole nor even the primary locus of Church activity and mission. Christian presence will always be communal, but it need not always be parochial. And the same must be true of diocesan structures. These boundaries need not always be territorial (the Military Ordinariate is the outstanding exception to the territorial pattern), but they should also follow the lines of professional or occupational concern. The bishop will always be the symbol of unity and the spokesman for various groupings of local communities (territorial or otherwise), just as the Pope will fulfill this role in relation to the international brotherhood of churches. What precise canonical or structural form these will take cannot be predicted easily at this early date. But one thing is fairly certain: whatever structures are assumed will themselves be subject to the continuing dialectic of change and development.

'Church Power'

It is becoming more fashionable nowadays to speak of the Christian community as a servant church. This has been common among certain Protestant and Anglican authors for the past few decades, but Catholics have only recently been influenced by their thought. The Second Vatican Council proposed, at least indirectly, a theology of the Servant Church, and Cardinal Cushing devoted his entire Advent Pastoral Letter of 1966 to this theme. I traced this development in Part I.

The risk is that all this talk about the Servant Church may remain just talk, that we shall all be satisfied with verbal victories and isolated symbols of change. The Servant Church is not necessarily a Church of Volkswagens rather than Cadillacs. This is a superficial approach to the problem. Indeed, there is a subtle danger inherent in this tendency to identify the Servant Church with this sort of 'stripping down' in the area of material goods and financial resources.

What does it profit the poor and the dispossessed if a bishop wears a cigar-band ring, or if the local pastor drives an old, run-down car, or if the Christian community celebrates the Eucharist in a barn rather than in a tastefully appointed church? If this were all it takes to refashion the Church into the Church of the Suffering Servant of God, then the task would be much easier than many people have thought. But this is as much an illusion as the conviction of some early 'liturgists' that rubrical adjustments and the demise of the lace surplice would bring a new day for the Church. The genuine leaders of the liturgical movement were too well grounded in theology to be satisfied with victories of that sort. These pioneers saw that liturgical renewal demanded nothing less than a complete radical rethinking of the theology of the Church, the sacraments, grace, the redemption, and so forth. History has, of course, vindicated these Christian visionaries.

So, too, suffering service does not mean wearing a ragged suit and unpolished shoes. This is the kind of narrow, individualistic spirituality that most proponents of the Servant Church would have deplored, under other circumstances. The issues are too grave to have us get bogged down in a Cadillac-or-Volkswagen controversy. If the Church in America is to become more fully the Church of the Suffering Servant of God, it must look around itself and outside of itself and see where the areas of division, hostility, injustice, tension, and illness lie. For the Church finds itself in a situation of great disparity between rich and poor, white and black, educated and illiterate. There is a real vacuum of power and influence between the large, so-called moderate elements of our society and the many who live on the fringes of our vast social structure.

The hippies, for example, have opted out of the 'normal' pattern of human behaviour because they can find no room for their ideals in the rat-race pace of contemporary American life. Whatever their faults they have become a kind of underground champion of so many traditional Christian values: peace, charity, justice, friendship, compassion. But they feel that the American society has become insensitive to these values, and is callously betraying them. The economically dispossessed are another case entirely. They are the poor, the illiterate, the unemployed, the homeless, the sick. They need power and money and articulate support. They need a vigorous, dedicated, and relentless lobbyist for their cause.

But the gap that exists between the hippies and the poor on the one hand, and the large middle-class moderates, on the other, is achingly wide. If the Church wants to play the role of servant, second-hand automobiles and cigar-band episcopal rings are not the path to follow. We are engaged in a massive program of self-deception if we think that this is what 'suffering service' is all about. The task of the Servant Church is more serious, more complex, and ultimately more Christian, than that. The Church must now be ready to place itself at the service of these social, political, economic, and cultural outcasts. Once more the Church must preach the good news to the poor by placing its immense moral, political, and financial resources at their disposal; by becoming, in other words, the bridge between the middle-class moderates and 'the other America'.

The Church must be the spokesman of the highest ideals of the Gospel, standing at the forefront in the struggle for peace, racial justice, and the alleviation of poverty, illiteracy, sickness, and all the evils of 'slum-ism'. This means that more of the Church's time, money, and energy will be spent on the building of God's Kingdom than on the building and maintenance of her own ecclesiastical plant. This simply is not true at the present time. 'Church power' is being harnessed for the sake of the Church, rather than for the sake of the Kingdom of God. And this will always be the case unless and until the Church accepts the Copernican and Einsteinian revolutions. The Church is not the Kingdom. It exists *for* the Kingdom, and for no other reason.

I am not suggesting here that the Christian community must enter the lists against these social evils precisely as the Christian community. There is no specifically ecclesiastical way of caring for orphans, the aged, or the sick. Religiously affiliated institutions, such as hospitals, can be justified in a situation where the civil authorities themselves have neither recognized nor responded adequately to these specific needs. In that case, the initiative of the Church accomplishes two ends: it stimulates the political government to reconsider the problem, and it provides temporary relief for the affected parties. As a third, indirect result, it also allows the Church to demonstrate its total commitment to the Gospel. Except in rare instances in the United States today, there is no reason why the Church should maintain and, what is worse, continue to build institutions of health, education, and welfare. There is a department in Washington which was created precisely for these purposes. The Church would best serve the needs of the human community, not by competing with or duplicating the services offered by the political community, but by donating its resources for their initial and continuing success. This would, by the way, relieve an extraordinary number of Church professionals from purely administrative work and allow them to devote themselves full time to the pastoral needs of the Christian community. Meanwhile, the nonprofessional in the Church could address himself wholeheartedly to the various social problems without asking himself whether or not he should carry on his work within the confines of Church-affiliated organizations.

The Magisterium, Theology, Heresy, and Conscience

The demand for serious theological reflection will exist as long as there is Christian faith, because theology is, in its simplest terms, 'faith seeking understanding' (St Anselm). And since Christian faith arises and is nourished from within the Christian community (see Rom 10:14–17), theology is the business of the Church as such. The theologian is, in the first instance, a Christian and a member of the Church. Within the Christian community he has a special job to do, and presumably he has the particular competence to perform it. His task is to develop an understanding of the faith in a systematic and coherent fashion and then to express this understanding through language which is at once clear, consistent, and intelligible.

As such, the theologian is a servant of the Church, and he provides his service in two ways: by exposition, explanation, and interpretation, on the one hand, and by radical criticism, on the other. First, the theologian must disclose the meaning of the Gospel by examining it in its original biblical setting, by tracing its development in the early Fathers of the Church and the great theologians of history, and by transmitting the significance and force of the various teachings of the Church, as expressed particularly in the ecumenical councils. The contemporary theologian would fulfill this first aspect of his servant function by explaining and interpreting, for example, the documents and decrees of the Second Vatican Council in order to bridge the gap between the theological advances made at Vatican II and the theological understanding of the so-called rank and file of the Christian community.

But the theologian cannot content himself with repeating or paraphrasing earlier teachings of the Church and assume that he has fulfilled his responsibility. The theologian must always be critical of the Church's teaching and preaching, of her spirituality and pastoral practice. This, too, is an essential part of his work. The Magisterium cannot execute this responsibility. It cannot preach and teach, and at the same time criticize its own proclamation and instruction. Moreover, the teaching Church would have little to teach if it were not for the theological work that precedes and follows all of her doctrinal formulations. It is not sufficient, therefore, that a theologian should spend all his time and effort offering a modest (and preferably moderate) commentary on the various council decrees or the latest papal encyclical. The Second Vatican Council is not the last word in theology. The council left much unsaid, and even said some things badly. It is one thing to bring the Church abreast of Vatican II, but it is quite another matter to bring the Church *beyond* Vatican II. The theologian must be able to engage in both tasks at the same time: exposition and explanation, on the one hand, and radical criticism, on the other.

It seems almost platitudinous to say it, but the really effective theologian is the one who can keep both tasks in proper balance. He does not serve the Church well if he becomes a mindless champion of the status quo, a so-called 'defender of orthodoxy', nor does he serve the community when he assumes the role of the habitual iconoclast, employing the knife of criticism for scarring rather than for healing. No theologian can escape this tension. On the contrary, today's theologian must dare to be wrong if he is to make any lasting contribution to the Church. All the Church asks is that he remain ever open to truth, wherever it may lead him and wherever he may find it. And the theologian asks in return that he be free to do his work without harassment (I do not say without criticism).

Does this mean that the Magisterium no longer has any

significant role to play in the understanding of Christian doctrine and that the dividing line between orthodoxy and heresy is blurred for all time? Let us consider the second question first.

The Code of Canon Law defines the heretic as a baptized person who, while retaining the name of Christian, pertinaciously denies or calls in doubt one of the truths that have to be believed with divine and Catholic faith (can. 1325, par. 2). Is this sort of heresy dead? It would seem, at first glance, that committal rites are long overdue. Despite the investigative efforts of the Vatican's Congregation for the Doctrine of the Faith in 1966–67, for instance, no heretics were brought to the light of public exposure (not even in the Netherlands). Moreover, an attitude of indifference regarding the truth or falsity of theological positions seems to prevail in some quarters of the Church today (Catholic and Protestant as well). Some are beginning to grow accustomed to ambiguity and disputation, and indifference has become the daughter of confusion.

In my judgment, the traditional notion of heresy, ossified in the Code, has indeed expired. Nevertheless, the Congregation for the Doctrine of the Faith has conducted its search within the restricted horizon of this canonical definition. No wonder that the heretics escaped detection. The rigid concept of heresy fails, in the first instance, to respect sufficiently the provisional and tentative character of dogmatic statements. The object of the Church's teaching is the mystery of our redemption in Christ. As a mystery, it is something radically inexhaustible, and therefore something that can never be described or defined adequately by human language alone. The doctrines of the Church will always be short of the mark. As such, they are always in need of reform and development, and are correspondingly open to varying theological interpretations.

Secondly, the traditional concept of heresy is too ideological and too verbal. The orthodox Catholic is the one who accepts the doctrinal 'party line'—without quarrel or quibble. The heretic is the one who denies such-and-such a doctrine, proposed by such-and-such a council or Pope, in such-and-such a century. But this kind of heresy is extremely rare in the life and history of the Church.

In recent years, theologians have begun to challenge the easy assumptions of this earlier notion of heresy. Karl Rahner has suggested that the pattern of heresy has changed today, that false religious doctrine is now a hidden and latent phenomenon. In fact, it may even coexist with verbal orthodoxy and an anxious, 'correct' care never to express views that might conflict with official doctrine.[3]

If one kind of heresy is, in fact, dead, then there is another type that continues to live. It is, on the one hand, more destructive of the unity of the Body of Christ, and on the other, more elusive and therefore more dangerous because it is (as Rahner suggests) something latent, implicit, and non-verbal. The contemporary heretic is not the one who denies the existence of angels or the usefulness of indulgences. These are minor, peripheral issues. The modern heretic may even appear spotlessly 'orthodox'. He perhaps would not think for a minute to deny or call into question the eternity of hell, the Virgin Birth, the infallibility of the Pope. And by the traditional definition of heresy, he cannot be faulted.

But ideological or verbal 'orthodoxy' sometimes masks a radical disorientation at the level that matters most: the very understanding of the Gospel itself. In point of fact, there are at least two major heresies prevalent in the American Church today: the one, for all practical purposes, denies the universality of God's redemptive love, and the other rejects the necessity of grace for salvation. The one denies the equality of men in the sight of God; the other insists that success is always the result of human initiative and enterprise and that failure is the fruit of human depravity. Both heresies are common in societies where widespread affluence makes the disparity between the haves and the have-nots greater than society itself can safely tolerate.

The first heresy is, of course, the doctrine of racism. This kind of prejudice denies the universality of God's call to the Kingdom. This is real heresy because it strikes at the very heart of the preaching and ministry of the Lord. As professed by a Christian, racism makes a mockery of baptism and the Eucharist.

The second distinctively American heresy is a form of rugged individualism. Those of us who firmly believe that people are poor because they are fundamentally lazy, because they will not work, or because they are neither clean nor moral, have opted for a strange mixture of Pelagianism (the heresy of 'self-help') and extreme Calvinism (the heresy of predestination, signified by economic success). Because of this heresy, millions of the poor are shut out by the theologically self-righteous indifference of the affluent.

This form of heresy cannot be eradicated by hierarchical edict, by the banning of books, or by the transfer of personnel. It can only be dissolved by conversion to the Gospel. And because the Church must always be a sign of God's Kingdom, she can never retreat from her posture of vigilance. Heresy is not dead. It lives in the 'Argentina' of an American value system which, in too many respects, saps the vitality of the Gospel of Jesus Christ.

If the theologian is to be accorded as much freedom as possible and if heresy is no longer a question of ideological deviation, then what is to be the specific place and function of the Magisterium of the Church? Our reflections in Chapter 7 in connection with the arguments of Charles Davis apply here as well. The Pope and bishops are symbols of unity and official spokesmen for the community. They are never independent of the community. The idea that the Pope or the body of bishops could define something or authoritatively proclaim something which is rejected by the overwhelming majority of the faithful is a theological fiction. The Magisterium is not above the community; it is an integral part of the community. It exists to provide the community with guidelines for its own self-understanding and to be a channel for the community's convictions and beliefs. The teaching of the Pope and bishops is authoritative insofar as it reflects and embodies the Gospel. If the teaching does not remain faithful to the Gospel or if it concerns matters which have only the most tenuous relationship to the Gospel, then the teaching has only as much authority as the reasonableness of the position can command. The authority, in other words, is intrinsic, not extrinsic. Such-and-such a teaching is not authoritative because an authority-figure has imposed it upon the Church. This teaching is authoritative, if at all, because it has behind it and actually contains the Word of God. In this regard, Martin Luther was right when he admitted the ecumenicity and even the infallibility of the early councils—insofar as their teaching was a faithful reflection of Sacred Scripture itself, which, in the final analysis, was the only infallible source of Christian truth.

In a pre-Copernican Church, doctrinal uniformity is exceedingly important. The Church exists for salvation. Men are saved if they believe the truth. The truth, in turn, is proclaimed and authentically interpreted by the Pope and bishops. Therefore, if one does not wish to jeopardize his salvation, he must adhere without qualification to whatever the Pope and bishops teach. Distinctions between infallible and noninfallible statements are meaningless. The benefit of the doubt is to be accorded to the magisterial pronouncement. After all, it might be right, even though noninfallible, in which case it is another of a long line of truths necessary for salvation.

But the issue of doctrinal orthodoxy assumes an entirely different perspective once the Copernican and Einsteinian revolutions have been assimilated. Because the Church is not primarily in the salvation business, ideological purity and uniformity is toward the bottom of her pastoral concerns. The only real heresy is the denial of the Gospel of love. Whether angels exist or whether Mary was a virgin *ante partum, in partu*, or *post partum* are essentially peripheral issues. But to the pre-Copernican mind, every tiny portion of the total corpus of Christian doctrine is equally vital. For if, indeed, angels do not exist, and if the Church has taught at one time that angels *do* exist, then the whole network loses its credibility.

The best example of this kind of thinking is the current discussion regarding the morality of contraception. The pre-Copernican has placed himself in the absolutist position of saying that if the Church does reverse her position on birth control, then the infallibility of her teaching and the authority of her Magisterium is lost. Accordingly, such a reversal of position would have an extraordinarily purifying effect on the contemporary Church.

The Copernican Revolution in ecclesiology demands that we take doctrinal orthodoxy (in the ideological, verbal sense) far less seriously. Salvation is not at stake. Christianity is not a new form of Gnosticism where adherence to certain secret truths (even when they have no apparent relation to reality) is the key to salvation. Besides, the Christian Church has remained remarkably unified in its understanding of the essentials of its faith, despite the fact that the greater portion of the Church is without any authoritative, magisterial guide at all.

Finally, the Einsteinian Revolution should lead us to expect as a matter of course, constant fluctuation in the Church's understanding of the faith. The Magisterium must try, as always, to reflect the actual consensus of the Church. And if the Pope and bishops are convinced that the consensus of the Church is moving in the wrong direction, then they have the obligation to attempt to create a new, countervailing consensus. If the Spirit is with them, the new consensus will eventually win the day. But the Pope and bishops never have the right to impose their own views on the Church without such an organic process. If, by chance, they do attempt to impose such a position, the Church itself will, and must, reject it.

If these reflections tend to deemphasize too much the role and authority of the Magisterium, this is my intention. The Pope and bishops have reserved to themselves far more authority than the New Testament or ecclesiology provide. If the lines of demarcation are not sufficiently clear, this is because the Einsteinian Revolution resists to the end any such attempts, arbitrary as they are, to impose absolute and clearly definable principles and distinctions. The Church itself, through its future experience, must sort out what is of enduring value and what is not. If we believe that the Church is the Body of Christ, as well as the sign and instrument of God's Kingdom, and that the Spirit of the Lord is with it until the consummation of the world, then there is no theological or pastoral reason to fear that the 'discernment of the Spirit' will be lacking. If there is any 'crisis of faith' in the Church today, it lies precisely with those who lose their nerve at this very point.

Conclusion

Do we need the Church? The answer seems to me to be clearly
'No' if by the Church we mean the Ptolemaic, pre-Ein-
steinian Church. Even traditional theology admits that men
can be saved apart from explicit membership in the Christian
community. The one norm of salvation is the living acceptance of the will of God (if only implicitly), and his will is
that we should have love one for another. Salvation comes
through participation in the Kingdom of God rather than
through affiliation with the Christian Church.

But the answer is clearly 'Yes' if, by the Church, we mean
the post-Copernican, post-Einsteinian Church. Christians
'need' this Church because it is the place where, by the choice
of God, they 'have been called into the fellowship of his Son,
Jesus Christ our Lord' (1 Cor 1:9) and through them 'spreads
the fragrance of the knowledge of him everywhere' (2 Cor
2:14). It is the place where, by divine election, they are
called upon to become both sign and instrument of the
Kingdom of God, i.e., of the human community as it
emerges in time and history under the sovereignty, judgment, and grace of the Gospel of Jesus Christ.

Non-Christians, too, 'need' the Church. Indeed, the whole
world 'needs' the Church, for the human community cannot
long survive without fidelity to what is essentially human and
criticism of what is fundamentally inhuman or antihuman.
Without criticism, freedom yields to totalitarianism, justice

gives way to exploitation, charity recedes into ruthlessness, peace dissolves into rivalry and hostility. The Church must offer itself as one of the principal agents whereby the human community is made to stand under the judgment of the enduring values of the Gospel of Jesus Christ: freedom, justice, peace, charity, compassion, reconciliation. The Church must be a place where all those forces, personal and political, which challenge and undermine these values are themselves effectively exposed, prophetically denounced, and, through the instrumentality of moral rather than material force, initially disarmed and dismantled.

The human community needs a Church which proclaims without compromise the dignity and worth of every person, lest he be swallowed up in society's technological jaws. It needs a Church which reminds us all of the fragile character of our existence and of our history, which bridles our arrogance, strips us of our pretentious self-images, and summons us to place everything under the judgment of God's Kingdom. The world needs a Church which offers itself and all its moral resources as the embodiment of charity and as one of charity's principal instruments. The world, in the final accounting, needs a Church which, as a revolutionary community, never rests until the principles of the Gospel of Jesus Christ are everywhere realized and extended.

But if the thesis of this book is wrong and if the Church is, in fact, primarily in the salvation business as understood by traditional theology, then I foresee little future for the Church as a vital instrument of God's Kingdom. If the Church continues to believe that it is the divinely appointed ordinary means of salvation and that all men are destined to belong to it, it will always be preoccupied with itself. Ecclesiology will always be a kind of theological narcissism. The Church will continue to hold the allegiance of conservative-minded people who are, by background and temperament, attracted by a 'religious' life. But the disengagement of all those who take history and politics seriously will continue at a rapidly increasing rate. There is no future for a Church which cares too little about the shape of the future, or about the welfare of the emerging human community.

The Church must subordinate its activities to the Kingdom of God. Unless the Gordian knot of Ptolemaic ecclesiology is cleanly severed, and unless the Copernican and Einsteinian revolutions are welcomed and fully embraced, the Church may find that it will encounter the gravest threat of its entire history, and this threat will originate with the many convinced Christians who will rise up in judgment against it and who will proceed to destroy it as a serious force in the world. I do not think this will come to pass, because I am convinced of the truth of the thesis and of the workings of the Spirit within the Body of Christ.

Notes

Preface and Introduction

1 New York: Herder & Herder and London: Burns & Oates, 1964 ff.

2 See the Second Vatican Council's *Decree on Ecumenism*, art. 3, para 1. Excerpts from the Constitutions of the Ecumenical Council are taken from *The Documents of Vatican II*, published by Guild Press, America Press, Association Press, and Herder & Herder, and copyrighted 1966 by The America Press. Used by permission. (New York, W. Abbott and J. Gallagher, eds. London: Geoffrey Chapman.)

3 *The Grave of God: Has the Church a Future?* N. D. Smith, trans. (New York: Harper & Row and London: Burns & Oates, 1967), p. 35.

4 *Ibid.*, p. 36.

5 New York: Doubleday, 1966. London: Muller, 1967.

6 New York: Trident Press, 1967. London: Hodder & Stoughton, 1968.

7 A more serious theological confrontation with the problem of the Church has been attempted by Rosemary Reuther in *The Church Against Itself* (New York: Herder & Herder, 1967), wherein the Church is identified with the eschatological community of faith, or the community of the new man. Such an eschatological perspective should restore the Christian community to the service of creation, releasing the Church into secularity and bringing to an end all religious otherworldliness. Unfortunately, the book is written from a passing theological perspective (Barthian dialecticism and Bultmannian existentialism) and there are many bibliographical lacunae. Mrs Reuther's argument would have been enhanced by direct confrontation with the thinking of Jürgen Moltmann, Ernst Bloch, Johannes Metz, Bishop John Robinson, Harvey Cox, Wolfhart Pannenberg, Rudolf Schnackenburg, and the later Bonhoeffer.

8 *Honest to God* (Philadelphia: Westminster, 1965 and London: Student Christian Movement Press, 1963), pp. 11, 13, and 27.

9 This is clearly the position adopted in the recent pastoral letter of the Catholic bishops of the United States, 'The Church in Our Day' (January 11, 1968).

Of course, I do not claim to be the first Catholic theologian to call this assumption into question. However, the scope of earlier studies has been more limited than mine. Thus, Heinz Schlette's *Towards a Theology of Religions* (New York: Herder & Herder and London: Burns & Oates, 1966) specifically disavows any attempt to deal meaningfully with the proposals of Bonhoeffer, Robinson, and others. 'I simply offer,' Schlette insists, 'a theological interpretation of non-Christian religions as tangible societies' (p. 12). Hans Küng has confronted the issue even more directly than Schlette, but his reflections are fashioned, as Schlette's, within the context of the relationship of Christianity and the non-Christian religions of the world. See 'The World Religions in God's Plan of Salvation,' *Christian Revelation and World Religions*, J. Neuner, ed. (London: Burns & Oates, 1967), pp. 25–66. Herein, Küng argues that the Church is better described as the 'extraordinary' rather than the 'ordinary' means of salvation. In this regard, I entirely agree with him, as the argumentation of this book will reveal. However, Küng concludes with the suggestion that the Church must invite and bring the other world religions from the status of *de jure* Christians to *de facto* Christians, from being Christians *in spe* to being Christians *in re*, from being Christians by designation and vocation to being Christians by profession and witness. Küng seems to return to the ecclesiocentric view which he criticizes earlier in his paper.

10 I should be clear at the outset what I mean by the Copernican and Einsteinian revolutions. I am using the terms analogously. Late medieval astronomy was Ptolemaic in character, i.e., it assumed that the earth is at the center of the universe and that all other heavenly bodies, including the sun, revolve around us. The position was challenged successfully by Nicolas Copernicus (1473–1543) who proposed the heliocentric theory, i.e. that the sun, and not the earth, is the center of celestial movement. In our argument, the Church is supplanted from the center of the history of salvation and replaced by the Kingdom of God. Similarly, the discoveries of Albert Einstein (1879–1955) have been employed in an analogous manner. Just as Copernicus launched his assault upon Ptolemaic astronomy, so did Einstein challenge Newtonian dynamics, which was based on the assumption that the laws of motion are the same with respect to all inertial frames of reference. Against the Newtonian assumption, Einstein posed the principle of relativity as a

fundamental general law of physics. Space and time are not absolutes, but relative to the frame of reference of a particular observer. In our argument, the structural components of the Church cannot be regarded as absolute in the Newtonian sense. History itself is creative of new forms and the Christian community's consciousness of itself as the Body of Christ grows and matures in the context of processive rather than static history. (See N. R. Hanson, 'Copernicus,' *The Encyclopedia of Philosophy*, P. Edwards, ed. (New York: Macmillan and Free Press and London: Collier–Macmillan, 1967), Vol. 2, pp. 219–22; and G. J. Whitrow, 'Einstein,' *ibid.*, pp. 468–71.)

11 Let me be clear as well about my understanding of 'secular theology', which will reappear throughout Part I. I do not limit the term to the work of Bonhoeffer, Robinson, Cox, and van Buren, nor do I regard it as a passing phase in Christian theology. I should be prepared to argue that the eschatological approach of Moltmann, Pannenberg, and Metz is genuinely secular in orientation, just as the secular theology of Robinson, for example, is radically eschatological. Both acknowledge the centrality of the Kingdom of God. Both see the future of the world in terms of the realization of this Kingdom. Therefore, I do not agree with Martin Marty's dismissal of 'secular theology' as having already made its fairly simple point: Jesus and the Church belong to and in the world. (See his review of Moltmann's *Theology of Hope* in *Critic* 26 (1968) 70–72.) The interrelationship of Jesus, Church, and world is an essentially eschatological question. And the eschatological orientation demands, as Metz himself suggests, a 'political theology'.

Chapter 1

1 John Macquarrie, *Principles of Christian Theology* (New York: Scribner's, 1966 and London: Student Christian Movement Press, 1967), p. 1.

2 *Evangelical Theology: An Introduction*, G. Foley, trans. (New York: Doubleday, 1964, and London: Weidenfeld & Nicolson, 1963), pp. 125–26. The emphasis is Barth's.

3 *The Secular City* (New York: Macmillan, 1965 and London: S.C.M. Press 1966), p. 17.

4. 'The Church and the World,' in *The Word in History*, T. Patrick Burke, ed. (New York: Sheed & Ward, 1966 and London: Collins, 1968), p. 72.

5 See his *Theology of Hope: On the Ground and the Implications of a Christian Eschatology*, J. W. Leitch, trans. (New York: Harper & Row and London: S.C.M. Press, 1967).

6 For a brief but useful introduction to Bloch, see S. Paul Schilling, 'Ernst Bloch: Philosopher of the Not-Yet', *Christian Century* 84 (1967) 1455–58.

7 'The Substance of Things Hoped For: An Interview with Harvey Cox on the Achievement of Ernst Bloch,' *Jubilee* 15 (1967) 9.

8 *Christianity and Crisis*, December 26, 1966, pp. 294–97.

9 *Ibid.*, p. 295.

10 *Pastoral Constitution on the Church in the Modern World*, art. 43.

11 See Richard Cardinal Cushing, *The Servant Church* (Boston: Daughters of St Paul, 1966), p. 10.

12 However, apart from some fleeting references in the writings of Metz and in the pastoral letter of Cardinal Cushing, in whose production the author participated, this central relationship has largely been ignored in Catholic ecclesiology.

My judgment is confirmed by the Lutheran theologian, Carl E. Braaten, who bemoans the fact that, while Protestant theology (via the works of Moltmann and Pannenberg) is rediscovering the eschatological, Kingdom-centered concept of the Church, Catholic theology has yet to move anywhere on the question. It is still lodged somewhere between the Body of Christ and the People of God images. Braaten views this condition as a matter of some ecumenical urgency. See his 'The Reunited Church of the Future,' *Journal of Ecumenical Studies* 4 (1967) 611–28, and 'The Church in Ecumenical and Cultural Cross-Fire,' *Theology Digest* 15 (1967) 283–94. K. E. Skydsgaard has expressed a similar concern in *Dialogue on the Way: Protestants Report from Rome on the Vatican Council*, G. A. Lindbeck, ed. (Minneapolis: Augsburg, 1965), pp. 167–74.

Hans Küng has called attention to the Church's subordination to the reign of God in his recent work, *The Church*, R. and R. Ockenden, trans. (New York: Sheed & Ward and London: Burns & Oates, 1968), pp. 43–104, but his orientation is, at times, strikingly close to Luther's *Alleinswirksamkeit Gottes* wherein the Kingdom is solely the work of God (see especially pp. 92 and 96). The influence of the Lutheran Rudolf Bultmann is evident throughout the discussion and there is, significantly, no meaningful reference to Moltmann, Pannenberg, Bloch, Metz, Chardin, Gogarten, or Bonhoeffer.

13 See K. Rahner, 'The Theological Position of Christians in the Modern World,' in *Christian Commitment* (New York and London:

Sheed & Ward, 1963); and Y. Congar, *Wide World My Parish*, D. Attwater, trans. (Baltimore: Helicon and London: Darton, Longman & Todd, 1961).

14 New York: Herder & Herder, 1966. London: Burns & Oates, 1967.

15 See my earlier book, *The Church in the Thought of Bishop John Robinson* (London: S.C.M. Press and Philadelphia: Westminster Press, 1966).

16 *Letters and Papers from Prison* (London: Collins, 1953), p. 91. All citations are from the Fontana edition, © S.C.M. Press.

17 Bonhoeffer's assessment of Barth has recently encountered criticism from two sides. Paul Lehmann challenges Bonhoeffer's critique of Barth's positivism of revelation in his essay, 'On Doing Theology: A Contextual Possibility,' in *Prospect for Theology: Essays in Honour of H. H. Farmer* F. G. Healey, ed. (London: Nisbet, 1966), p. 129. And, from an opposite direction, Peter Berger dismisses the basis for Barth's distinction between 'religion' and 'Gospel', a distinction which Bonhoeffer endorses. See *The Sacred Canopy: Elements of a Sociological Theory of Religion* (New York: Doubleday, 1967), esp. pp. 179–88, see also 'A Sociological View of the Secularization of Theology,' *Journal for the Scientific Study of Religion* 6 (1967) 3–16.

18 According to J. A. Phillips, 'the sharing in the sufferings of God' represents the consummation of Bonhoeffer's theology. See *Christ for Us in the Theology of Dietrich Bonhoeffer* (New York: Harper & Row and London [with the title: *The form of Christ in the World*]: Collins, 1967), p. 221 and all of chap. 16. The new Dutch Catechism is also instructive on this point. See *A New Catechism: Catholic Faith for Adults*, K. Smyth, trans. (New York: Herder & Herder and London: Burns & Oates, 1967), pp. 492–502.

19 See also his *Christ the Center*, J. Bowden, trans. (New York: Harper & Row and London [with the title: *Christology*]: Collins, 1966), with an Introduction by Edwin H. Robertson.

20 The phenomenon of Bonhoeffer's special popularity among Catholics has been analyzed recently by W. Kuhns, 'A Catholic Looks at Bonhoeffer,' *Christian Century* 84 (1967) 830–32. See also his *In Pursuit of Dietrich Bonhoeffer* (Dayton, Ohio: Pflaum Press, 1967 and London: Burns & Oats, 1968).

21 *The Place of Bonhoeffer*, M. Marty, ed. (New York: Association Press, 1962, and London: S.C.M. Press, 1963), p. 10.

22 It should be noted that two sympathetic critics, Albert Van den Heuvel and Paul van Buren, faulted Robinson's order of argumentation.

(See Van den Heuvel's 'The Honest to God Debate in Ecumenical Perspective,' *Ecumenical Review* 16 (1964) 279–94; and Van Buren's *Secular Meaning of the Gospel* (New York: Macmillan, 1963, and London: S.C.M. Press, 1965), p. 200, n. 5.) Both agreed, independently of one another, that the problem of God should have been placed within the larger and more immediate context of the problem of the Christian life and the place of Christ. Robinson abides by this criticism in his next book—*The New Reformation?*—wherein his pastoral (or ecclesiological) interests come through in unmistakably clear terms.

23 See *Honest to God*, chaps. 5 and 6.

24 New York: Harper & Row, 1963, 1964, and 1967.

25 This is said without discounting the potential contribution of American theologians outside the 'secular' tradition, e.g., the above-mentioned J. M. Robinson, J. Cobb, also Herbert Richardson. See the latter's *Toward an American Theology* (New York: Harper & Row, 1967).

Furthermore, in speaking here of the 'Americanization' of the discussion, I do not mean to imply that the concerns of Cox or the 'death-of-God' theologians are strictly European in origin. Harvey Cox was not the first American theologian to explore and to highlight the secular dimension of the Kingdom of God. This secular orientation has been in our national tradition for some time, as the classic work of H. R. Niebuhr amply suggests. (See *The Kingdom of God in America* [New York: Harper & Row, 1937; Torchbook ed., 1959]. For a more recent historical survey, see S. E. Ahlstrom's *Theology in America: The Major Protestant Voices from Puritanism to Neo-Orthodoxy* [Indianapolis: Bobbs-Merrill, 1967], pp. 23–91.) On the other hand, we have to be careful about drawing easy parallels, particularly with regard to the social gospel tradition of Walter Rauschenbusch. Cox has specifically rejected the suggestion that the present discussion in contemporary American theology is nothing more than a repristination of the social gospel. (See *The Secular City Debate*, D. Callahan, ed. [New York: Macmillan, 1966, and London: Collier-Macmillan 1967], p. 88.)

26 Criticism of Harvey Cox's theology of secularity is available in *The Secular City Debate*, D. Callahan, ed. (New York: Macmillan, 1966); in John Bennett's essay, 'The Church and the Secular,' to which I have already referred; and in Robert Adolfs' *The Grave of God* (see Introduction, n. 3), wherein he raises two interesting questions about the new secular theology. In the first place, has the proposition that secularization is demanded by Christian revelation and is, in fact, a consequence of the preaching of the biblical message been vindicated

adequately? Are the theological arguments entirely convincing? Secondly, have these theologians not perceived the growing power of secularism in a hidden and new form within the structures of our society, and have they consequently failed to provide a sufficient analysis of the true situation?' (see p. 89).

27 Rev. ed.; New York: Association Press, and London: Darton, Longman & Todd, 1966.

28 See his *Radical Theology and the Death of God*, with T. J. J. Altizer (Indianapolis: Bobbs-Merrill, 1966), p. 7. (Harmondsworth: Penguin Books, 1968.)

29 See my article, 'Radical Theology: From Honest-to-God to God-is-Dead,' *Commonweal* 84 (1966) 605–8.

30 The late Robert L. Richard, S.J., has provided a sympathetic survey and analysis of some contemporary secular theologians, such as Robinson, Cox, and Van Buren, in his *Secularization Theology* (New York: Herder & Herder, 1967). Father Richard's discussion is limited to the first question, the secular meaning of the Gospel, and barely touches upon the problem of the Church. Consequently, his work, useful as it may be in itself, is not directly pertinent to the thesis of this book.

31 See Metz's essay, 'The Church and the World' (cited above, n. 4), which provides a summary and synthesis of his current thinking, and also his 'Relationship of Church and World in the Light of a Political Theology,' in *Theology of Renewal*, Vol. II, L. K. Shook, ed. (New York: Herder & Herder, 1968), pp. 255–70.

32 New York: Herder & Herder, 1966.

Chapter 2

1 C. E. Schaldenbrand, trans. (New York: Desclee, 1966).

2 *Letters and Papers from Prison*, p. 166.

3 Philadelphia: Westminster Press, 1965.

4 Robert Adolfs gives Robinson proper credit for offering the most radical attitude toward the way of the Church in contemporary theological writing. See *The Grave of God*, p. 117.

5 John A. T. Robinson, *On Being the Church in the World* (London: S.C.M. Press, 1960), p. 20.

6 Robinson, *The New Reformation?* (Philadelphia: Westminster Press and London: S.C.M. Press, 1965) p. 36.

7 *Ibid.*, p. 46.

8 *On Being the Church in the World*, p. 145.

9 *The New Reformation?* pp. 46–47.

10 *Honest to God*, p. 134.

11 *Ibid.*, p. 139.

12 *Ibid.*, p. 134.

13 *The New Reformation?* p. 99. For a fuller summary of Robinson's ecclesiology, see my earlier work, *The Church in the Thought of Bishop John Robinson* (see chap. 1, n. 15) chap. 5, pp. 97–108.

14 *The Secular City*, p. 125.

15 See 'Kingdom, Church and Ministry,' in *The Historic Episcopate*, K. M. Carey, ed. (2d ed.; London: Dacre Press, 1960), p. 16.

16 Reference has already been made, however briefly, to the ecclesiological views of Van Buren and Hamilton. I am limiting the discussion here to Thomas Altizer's *The Gospel of Christian Atheism* (Philadelphia: Westminster Press, 1966, and London: Collins, 1967).

17 *Ibid.*, pp. 9–10.

18 *Ibid.*, p. 12.

19 Philadelphia: Westminster, 1963.

20 *Mircea Eliade*, pp. 13–14.

21 See *The Gospel of Christian Atheism*, p. 26.

22 *Ibid.*, pp. 132–33.

23 'A Theological Interpretation . . .,' in *Christian Commitment* (see chap. 1, n. 13), p. 20.

24 Eugene Hillman, C.S.Sp., has attempted to develop a missiology in the spirit of Karl Rahner. See his *The Church as Mission* (New York: Herder & Herder, 1965, and London: Sheed & Ward, 1966). Hillman argues that the Church is not simply a means of salvation but it must also be a sign of salvation among all peoples, 'among the distinctive ethnic-culture units of people who make up mankind' (p. 38). The Church's task in these last days is to preach the Gospel and to establish itself everywhere as the visible sacrament of Christ. And once the Church has accomplished this task, human history will have been completed and the Lord will come again. It should be evident, as I develop my own theological argument throughout this book, that Hillman's position is far less extensive and far less radical than my own. Although he is overtly indebted to Karl Rahner, the orientation of his work is closer to the kerygmatic tradition in Christian theology (e.g., Oscar Cullmann) and, consequently, more directly opposed to the thesis of my book than might be apparent at first glance. My disagreement with Jean Daniélou is even more obvious. See Daniélou's *Prayer as a Political Problem*, J. R. Kirwan, trans. (New York: Sheed & Ward and London: Burns & Oates, 1967).

25 *Wide World My Parish* (see chap. 1, n. 13), p. 12.

26 See his *Christ the Sacrament of Encounter with God* (New York and London: Sheed & Ward, 1963); also his essay, 'The Church and Mankind,' in *Concilium* 1 (January, 1965) 34–49.

27 See 'Sanctity, a sign of revelation,' *Theology Digest* 15 (1967) 41–46.

Chapter 3

1 See, for example, J. C. Hoekendijk, *The Church Inside Out*, W. L. Jenkins, trans. (Philadelphia: Westminster, 1966 and London: S.C.M. Press, 1967), especially pp. 42–43. A more significant example is offered by Jürgen Moltmann, who insists that the Church's 'existence is completely bound to the fulfilling of its service. For this reason it is nothing in itself, but all that it is, it is in existing for others.' (*Theology of Hope* [see chap. 1, n. 5], p. 327.)

2 J. A. Phillips argues that Christology is the key to understanding Bonhoeffer's thought: *Christ for Us in the Theology of Dietrich Bonhoeffer* (see chap. 1, n. 18). E. H. Robertson concurs with Phillips's judgment: see 'Bonhoeffer's Christology' in *Christ the Center* (chap. 1, n. 19), p. 10.

3 Bonhoeffer, *Christ the Center*, p. 40.

4 *Ibid.*, pp. 60–61.

5 *Ibid.*, p. 65. That pre-Copernican ecclesiology is 'ecumenical' in dimension is evident in the theology of Oscar Cullmann. He, too, refers to the Church as 'the center, the mid-point from which Christ exercises his invisible lordship over the whole world. It is not only a part, but the heart.' *The Christology of the New Testament*, S. Guthrie and C. Hall, trans. (rev. ed.; Philadelphia: Westminster, 1963), p. 229. London: S.C.M. Press, 1959, p. 229.

6 Rudolf Schnackenburg, *The Church in the New Testament*, W. J. O'Hara, trans. (New York: Herder & Herder and London: Burns & Oates, 1965), p. 9.

7 Charles Journet's *The Church of the Word Incarnate*, A. Downes, trans. (New York and London: Sheed & Ward, 1955), comes closest to such an effort, but it is inextricably bound up with scholastic categories and, in the end, fails to meet the need. One of the best single-volume biblical ecclesiologies is provided by Father Schnackenburg in the title just mentioned above.

8 Schnackenburg, *op. cit.*, p. 165.

9 See H. Schlier, *Christus und die Kirche im Epheserbrief* (Tübingen: Mohr-Siebeck, 1930); E. Käsemann, *Leib und Leib Christi: Beiträge zur historischen Theologie* (Tübingen: Mohr-Siebeck, 1933); and M. Dibelius, *An die Thessalonicher 1–2, an die Philipper* (3 ed.; Tübingen: Mohr-Siebeck, 1937), esp. pp. 85–93.

10 *Theology of the New Testament*, K. Grobel, trans. (London: S.C.M. Press, 1955), Vol. II, p. 299.

11 *The Church in the Theology of St Paul*, G. Webb and A. Walker, trans. (New York: Herder & Herder and London: Nelson, 1959), pp. 343–44.

12 'Corps, Tête et Plérôme dans les épîtres de la Captivité,' *Revue Biblique* 63 (1956) 5–44.

13 *The Body: A Study in Pauline Theology* (London: S.C.M. Press, 1952), p. 47.

14 *Ibid.*, p. 50, n. 1.

15 *Ibid.*, p. 51.

16 *The Church and the Sacraments*, W. J. O'Hara, trans. (New York: Herder & Herder and London: Burns & Oates, 1963), pp. 18–19.

17 But see *The Interpretation of the Fourth Gospel* (Cambridge, Eng.: The University Press, 1963), p. 447, n. 1, where Dodd suggests that the term 'realized eschatology' does not exactly express his position.

18 A summary of the Protestant discussion has been provided by Norman Perrin, *The Kingdom of God in the Teaching of Jesus* (Philadelphia: Westminster, 1963, and London: S.C.M. Press, 1966).

19 'History and Eschatology in the New Testament,' *New Testament Studies* 1 (1954–5) 16.

20 Rudolf Bultmann, *Jesus Christ and Mythology* (London: S.C.M. Press, 1960), pp. 25–26.

21 *Ibid.*, p. 81.

22 *Ibid.*, pp. 82–83.

23 C. H. Dodd, *The Parables of the Kingdom* (rev. ed.; London: Collins, 1961), p. 152; see also *The Apostolic Preaching and its Developments* (New York: Harper & Row, 1962 and London: Hodder & Stoughton, 1963), pp. 94–95.

24 'Christ, Creation and the Church,' in *The Background of the New Testament and Its Eschatology*, W. D. Davies and D. Daube, eds. (Cambridge, Eng.: The University Press, 1956), p. 422.

25 See his essay, 'The Kingship of Christ and the Church in the New

Testament,' in *The Early Church*, A. J. B. Higgins, ed. (London: S.C.M. Press, 1956), pp. 105–37.

26 *Ibid.*, p. 116.

27 *Ibid.*, p. 123.

28 *Ibid.*, p. 126.

29 Oscar Cullmann, *Christ and Time*, F. Filson, trans. (rev. ed.; London: S.C.M. Press, 1962), p. 154.

30 Wolfhart Pannenberg, 'Theology and the Kingdom of God,' *Una Sancta* 24, no. 2 (1967) 5. Similar criticisms have been formulated by J. Moltmann in *Theology of Hope* (see chap. 1, n. 5), pp. 37–76. Moltmann also criticizes Pannenberg's notion of revelation through history. See pp. 76–84.

31 'The Kingdom of God and the Church,' *Una Sancta* 24, no. 4 (1967) 3–27.

32 See his *Aspects nouveaux du problème de l'Église* (Fribourg: Librairie de l'Université, 1941), pp. 166–7.

33 *God's Rule and Kingdom*, J. Murray, trans. (London: Nelson, 1963), pp. 233–34.

34 *Ibid.*, p. 313.

35 *On Being the Church in the World* (see chap. 2, n. 5), p. 20.

36 'Kingdom, Church and Ministry' (see chap. 2, n. 15), p. 15.

37 From the Foreword to *The Church in the Thought of Bishop John Robinson* (see chap. 1, n. 15), p. x.

38 Cushing, *The Servant Church* (see chap. 1, n. 11), p. 6.

39 The theological tension between the 'already' and the 'not yet' has been proposed on several occasions throughout this book. However, I should not want to be interpreted as having endorsed the static concept of history whereby the end is already predetermined, the Kingdom is already prepared, the success of history is already assured. History can fail. It is the Christian hope that history will not fail if men co-operate with God as he summons us to the task of constructing the Kingdom of God here and now, amidst the political, economic, cultural, and scientific ambiguities of human existence and human history. The tension between the 'already' of the resurrection and the 'not yet' of the second coming is useful and should not be discounted arbitrarily. But Oscar Cullmann's understanding of this tension tends to be simplistic and needs to be complemented by the more recent criticisms of Pannenberg, Bloch, and Moltmann. So, too, must Cullmann's schema be balanced off with the evolutionary, processive concept of history proposed with some measure of success and illumination by Teilhard de Chardin.

Chapter 4

1 *Christ and Church* (see chap. 2, n. 1), p. 83.

2 The patristic stress on the identification of Christ and the Church accounts, in large part, for the traditional Catholic emphasis in this direction. However, it should always be noted that the Fathers never divorced this identification from the basic theological notion of Mystery. The Church is the sacrament of Christ, but never simply a juridically organized, hierarchically structured 'perfect society'. See, for example, the first chapter of the Second Vatican Council's *Dogmatic Constitution on the Church*, where the biblical and patristic emphasis on the Mystery comes through clearly.

3 *Lay People in the Church*, D. Attwater, trans. (Westminster, Md.: Newman, 1959), p. 39. (London: Chapman, rev. ed. 1964.)

4 *De controversiis*, Vol. II, bk. 3, chap. 2 (Naples: 1857), p. 74.

5 Father Tromp's work is available in English translation in *Corpus Christi Quod est Ecclesia*, A. Condit, trans. (New York: Vantage Press, 1960).

6 *Ibid.*, p. 19.

7 *Ibid.*, p. 20.

8 *Ibid.*, p. 23.

9 *Idem.*

10 *Idem.*

11 *Ibid.*, p. 24.

12 *Idem.*

13 *Ibid.*, p. 172.

14 *Ibid.*, p. 195.

15 *Ibid.*, p. 196.

16 From an encyclical letter of Pope Pius X, *Vehementer Nos, Acta Apost. Sedis* 39 (1906) 8.

17 *Corpus Christi*, p. 198.

18 *Ibid.*, p. 210.

19 I say this despite what some otherwise discerning commentators have written in praise of *Mystici Corporis*. For example, see J. Hamer, O.P., *The Church Is a Communion*, R. Matthews, trans. (New York: Sheed & Ward and London: Chapman, 1964), pp. 13 ff., and, surprisingly, Robert Adolfs, *The Grave of God* (see Introduction, n. 3), p. 100.

20 See his *Ekklesiologie im Werden* (Paderborn: Drückerei, 1940), p. 122.

21 *Acta Apostolicae Sedis* (AAS) 35 (1943) 199.

22 H. Denzinger, *Enchiridion Symbolorum Definitionum et Declarationum de Rebus Fidei et Morum,* K. Rahner, ed. (Freiburg: Herder, 1956), 2319.

23 *AAS* 35 (1943) 197.

24 *Ibid.,* p. 199.

25 *Ibid.,* p. 224.

26 *Ibid.,* p. 234.

27 *Ibid.,* p. 199.

28 *Ibid.,* p. 204.

29 *Ibid.,* pp. 202–3.

30 *Ibid.,* pp. 217 ff.; 226–27.

31 *Ibid.,* pp. 231 ff.

32 *Ibid.,* pp. 215 ff.

33 *Ibid.,* p. 201.

34 *Ibid.,* pp. 219–20.

35 *Ibid.,* p. 199.

36 The full English text is available in *The American Ecclesiastical Review* 77 (1952) 307–11.

37 See R. Adolfs, *The Grave of God,* pp. 104 ff.

38 See, for example, the chapter 'Salvation through the Church,' in H. de Lubac's *Catholicism: A Study of the Corporate Destiny of Mankind* (New York: Sheed & Ward, 1958 and London: Burns & Oates, 1962), pp. 107–125.

39 From the Foreword to *The Church in the Thought of Bishop John Robinson,* p. x.

Chapter 5

1 Such commentaries are already available. See, for example, *The Documents of Vatican II,* W. Abbott and J. Gallagher, eds. (New York: Guild, America, and Association Presses and London: Chapman, 1966).

2 Full-length, popular commentaries on *Lumen Gentium* are also available. See, for example, George Tavard, *The Pilgrim Church* (New York: Herder & Herder and London: Burns & Oates, 1967).

3 New York and London: Sheed & Ward, 1963, p. 48.

4 See also Karl Rahner, *The Church and the Sacraments,* W. J. O'Hara, trans. (New York: Herder & Herder and London: Burns & Oates, 1963).

5 A fuller discussion of 'mystery' is proposed by M. J. LeGuillou, *Christ and Church* (see chap. 2, n. 1). A popular summary of recent scholarship is provided by J. McKenzie, *Dictionary of the Bible* (Milwaukee: Bruce, 1965, and London: Chapman, 1966), pp. 595–8.

6 Charles Moeller, 'History of Lumen Gentium's Structure and Ideas' in *Vatican II: An Interfaith Appraisal*, J. H. Miller, ed. (South Bend, Ind.: University of Notre Dame Press, 1966), p. 126.

7 *The Church in the New Testament*, W. J. O'Hara, trans. (New York: Herder & Herder, 1965), p. 189.

8 *Peter: Disciple, Apostle, Martyr* (New York: Meridian, 1958), p. 204. London: S.C.M. Press, rev. ed., 1966, p. 210.

9 *Op. cit.*, p. 191.

10 *God's Rule and Kingdom* (see chap. 3, n. 33), p. 258.

11 Unfortunately, the pastoral letter of the United States Catholic Bishops, 'The Church in Our Day' (January, 1968) presses the distinction between priest and people even further than Vatican II had done, failing even to admit that both ordained and nonordained share in the one priesthood of Christ.

12 *Power and Poverty in the Church* (Baltimore: Helicon and London: Chapman, 1964), p. 137.

13 Schnackenburg, *The Church in the New Testament*, p. 149.

14 *The Mystery of the Temple*, R. F. Trevett, trans. (Westminster, md.: Newman and London: Burns & Oates, 1962), p. ix.

15 *Ibid.*, pp. 236–37.

16 *Vatican II: An Interfaith Appraisal*, pp. 126–27.

17 *Ibid.*, p. 127.

Chapter 6

1 The decree uses here a phrase from the Holy Office letter to Cardinal Cushing, of Boston.

2 Art. 1, para. 2 and 3.

3 See R. E. Brown, *The Gospel According to John*, 'Anchor Bible Series' (New York: Doubleday, 1966), pp. 141–44.

4 *God Who Acts: Biblical Theology as Recital* (London: S.C.M. Press, 1952), pp. 50–51.

5 See H. H. Rowley, *The Biblical Doctrine of Election* (London: Lutterworth Press, 1950). The question is discussed in a more popular

and synthetic manner by J. McKenzie, *Dictionary of the Bible* (see above, chap. 5, n. 5), p. 227.

6 Even Karl Rahner in his essay, 'Membership of the Church According to the Teaching of Pius XII's Encyclical "Mystici Corporis Christi"' (*Theological Investigations*, Vol. II, K. Kruger, trans. [Baltimore: Helicon and London: Darton, Longman & Todd, 1963], pp. 36 ff.) attempts a defense of this convenient construct.

7 *Vatican II: An Interfaith Appraisal*, p. 201.

8 *Theological Investigations*, Vol. II, p. 84.

9 *Ibid.*, p. 85.

10 *Vatican II: An Interfaith Appraisal*, pp. 204–205.

11 *Theological Dictionary*, with H. Vorgrimler (New York: Herder & Herder, 1965 and London: Burns & Oates, 1966), p. 419.

12 *The Council and Reunion* (London: Sheed & Ward, 1961), p. 215.

Chapter 7

1 *Belief and Unbelief: A Philosophy of Self-Knowledge* (New York: Macmillan, 1965, and London: Darton, Longman & Todd, 1966), p. 192.

2 John Macquarrie, *Principles of Christian Theology* (see chap. 1, n. 1), p. 75.

3 My position, therefore, is not to be confused with Karl Rahner's. At the conclusion of a lecture given at Boston College (October 29, 1967), Rahner was asked, 'If the offer of salvation is made to all mankind, even atheists, what advantage does explicit Christianity offer?' Rahner used an analogy to explain his position. A small child could very well ask himself the question, 'I am already a man, so what sense does it make to grow up? I may just as well die now because, if I do grow up, I will never be more than a man, which is what I am now.' The child is the implicit Christian and the full-grown man is the explicit Christian. To reject explicit Christianity, even when it can be accepted, is to reject human growth and maturity.

I disagree with this point of view because it does not seem to take into adequate account the biblical doctrine of election. To adopt Rahner's position is to assume that God, by the free gift of his election, offers some few men a greater opportunity for human growth and maturity than he offers to others.

4 John A. T. Robinson, *Honest to God* (see Introduction, n. 8), p. 134.

5 'Kingdom, Church and Ministry,' in *The Historic Episcopate* (see chap. 1, n. 43), p. 16.

6 See *A Question of Conscience* (New York: Harper & Row and London: Hodder & Stoughton, 1967), p. 190.

7 *Ibid.*, p. 42. Fr Gregory Baum has attempted such a response in *The Credibility of the Church Today: A Reply to Charles Davis* (New York: Herder & Herder, 1968), esp. pp. 121–76.

8 See *ibid.*, pp. 62–126.

9 See Part III of this book, pp. 145–8.

10 See *op. cit.*, pp. 126–78.

11 See H. Küng, ' "Early Catholicism" in the New Testament as a Problem in Controversial Theology,' *The Council in Action: Theological Reflections on the Second Vatican Council*, C. Hastings, trans. (New York: Sheed & Ward, 1963), pp. 159–95. London: Sheed & Ward, 1963, with the title *The Living Church*, pp. 233–293.

12 See, for example, J. McKenzie, *Authority in the Church* (New York: Sheed & Ward and London: Chapman, 1966). For a more systematic discussion cf. H. Küng's *The Church* (see chap. 1, n. 12), pp. 70–79, 363–480, *et passim*.

13 See Davis's comments, *op. cit.*, pp. 97–103.

14 *Lumen Gentium*, art. 8.

15 For an important discussion of the problem of papal jurisdiction, see H. Marot, 'The Primacy and the Decentralization of the Early Church,' *Concilium* 7 (September, 1965) 9–16. Rome's assertion of its primacy did not reach Vatican I proportions until the fifth century. Marot demonstrates that there was real structural variety in the early Church and that this variety did not conflict with the primacy of Rome. Structural pluralism disappeared after about ten centuries because of a purely incidental application of this primacy in a way which occasionally obscured its true significance. This change occurred with the extension of the granting of the pallium, the symbol of episcopal authority. The Council of the Lateran in 1215 decreed that the heads of the patriarchates could confer the pallium on the bishops under their jurisdiction only after receiving the pallium from the Pope and after having taken an oath of allegiance and obedience. Thus, by means of the pallium, patriarchal and other jurisdictions were considered as a kind of emanation of, and participation in, the *plentitudo potestatis* reserved exclusively to the Pope. 'But this centralizing tendency,' Marot argues, 'going beyond historical contingencies, was linked, as in the West,

with the views of a "Roman school" inspired by the medieval papacy. It was not the result of teaching of the primacy which remained throughout the centuries wholly compatible with the existence of three very differently organized zones within the universal Church' (p. 14).

See also the historical findings of Brian Tierney: *Foundations of the Conciliar Theory* (Cambridge, Eng.: The University Press, 1955); 'Ockham, the Conciliar Theory and the Canonists,' *Journal of the History of Ideas* 15 (1954) 40–70; 'Pope and Council: Some New Decretist Texts,' *Medieval Studies* 19 (1957) 197–218; 'Canon Law and Western Constitutionalism,' *Catholic Historical Review* 52 (1966) 1–17; 'Hermeneutics and History: The Problem of *Haec Sancta*,' *Essays in Honor of Bertie Wilkinson* (Toronto: 1967).

See also A. Franzen, 'The Council of Constance: Present State of the Problem,' *Concilium* 7 (1965) 29–68.

16 Denzinger-Bannwaert 1839 (see chap. 4, n. 22).

17 *Op. cit.*, p. 161.

18 On July 29, 1968, after this book had already gone to press, Pope Paul VI did finally issue an encyclical letter, *Humanae Vitae*, in which he reaffirmed the earlier prohibitive teaching, but without laying claim to infallibility. A critical response to the encyclical is contained in the statement of various American Catholic theologians (including myself), released at the Catholic University of America, Washington, D.C., on the following day.

19 *Ibid.*, p. 124.

20 *Lumen Gentium*, art. 50.

21 See Gabriel Moran, *Theology of Revelation* (New York: Herder & Herder, 1966). I have not specifically incorporated Moltmann's eschatological understanding of revelation in this particular section. My purposes here are limited to the question: How should the call to membership in the Church be issued? It should be clear by now, however, that Moltmann's notion of revelation as *promise* is consonant with the general thesis of this book. I have already made some reference to it in the discussion of J. B. Metz (see chap. I, pp. 52–55).

22 See *The Idea of History* (New York: Galaxy, 1956).

23 For an introduction to the problem of apologetics and biblical studies, see Avery Dulles, S.J. *Apologetics and the Biblical Christ* (Westminster, Md.: Newman and London: Burns & Oates, 1964).

Chapter 8

1 As a general rule, however, baptism should be administered to infants and young children only when there is a reasonable certainty that they will be educated in the Christian faith, and, therefore, have the option of accepting and executing the mission of the Church as communicated through the sacrament. Merely formal incorporation into the Church is to be consistently rejected.

2 See Karl Rahner, 'Theology of the Parish,' in *The Parish: From Theology to Practice*, H. Rahner, ed. (Westminster, Md.: Newman, 1958), p. 28.

3 See *On Heresy* (New York: Herder & Herder and London: Burns & Oates, 1964); see also J. Macquarrie, 'Some Thoughts on Heresy,' *Christianity and Crisis*, December 26, 1966, and J. Finnegan, 'The Secular Meaning of Heresy,' *The Ecumenist* (May–June, 1967). See also the report of the Advisory Committee of the Episcopal Church, *Theological Freedom and Social Responsibility*, S. Bayne, ed. (New York: Seabury Press, 1967).

INDEX

Index